# ENJOY LEARNING BIOCHEMISTRY

## QUESTIONS ANSWERS FROM BIOCHEMISTRY

RAHUL MESHRAM

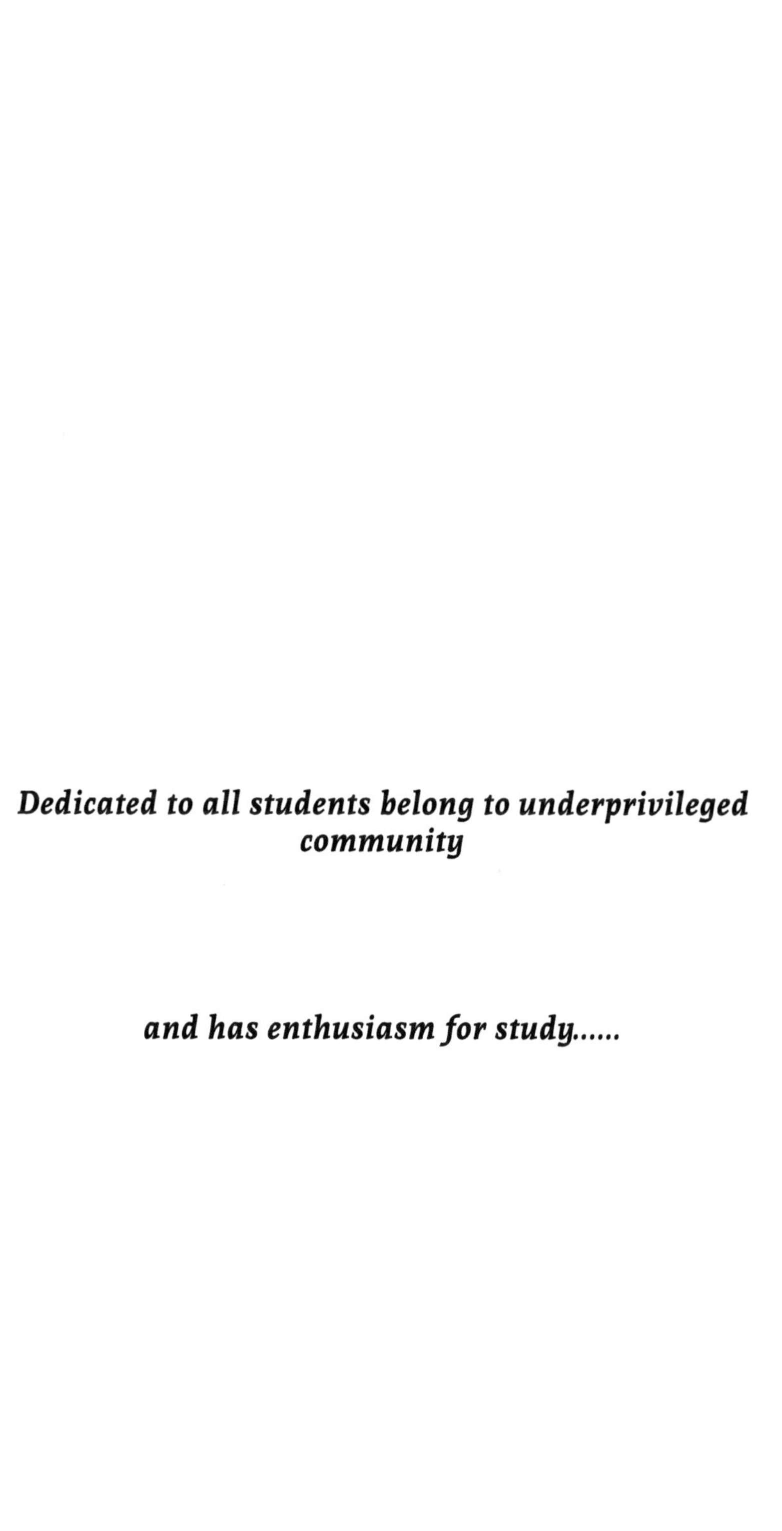

*Dedicated to all students belong to underprivileged community*

*and has enthusiasm for study......*

# Contents

# Preface

This book provides basic concepts not only for UG and PG students of Biochemistry course, but it also give an opportunity for students from Diploma and degree in Pharmacy, Medical Laboratory Technology, Nursing, Home science, Nutritional Biochemistry background to understand and learn the biochemical concepts lucidly.

Formats of the book is in question answer manner that doesn't put burden of topics and students also enjoy learning biochemistry gradually and stepwise fashion. Books cover basics of carbohydrates, fats, protein, nucleic acids and also explain metabolism of these biomolecules. Concepts of enzyme, coenzyme, with classification and application also covered in the book. Ideas of hormones and their biological role with structural details with basic concepts of blood and clotting mechanism make this book a brief and concise guide for naïve students entering in biochemistry arena.

Students from Home science always feel the need for the book which acquaint them with introductory and basic concept of biochemistry, and I think this book fulfill their wish.

Enjoy learning BIOCHEMISTRY..................

SACHIN C NARWADIYA, RAHUL L MESHRAM, DAMINI R MOTWANI

Date 04-04-2022

# ACKNOWLEDGEMENTS

First and foremost, praises and thanks to the God, the Almighty, for His showers of blessings throughout the book writing work to complete a good book successfully.

We would like to express my deep and sincere gratitude to Sindhu Mahavidyalaya Principal for his enourgaement to write a nice piece of work in Biochemistry providing invaluable guidance. His dynamism, vision, sincerity, and motivation have deeply inspired us. He has taught me the methodology to carry out the research and to present the research works as clearly as possible. We are extremely grateful for what he has offered to us. We would also like to thank him for his friendship, empathy, and great sense of humor.

Finally, our thanks go to all the people who have supported me to complete the for writing this book directly or indirectly.

SACHIN C NARWADIYA , RAHUL L MESHRAM , DAMINI R MOTWANI

# I

# Carbohydrate

**What are carbohydrates?**

**Ans**- Carbohydrate are polyhydroxy derivatives of aldehydes & ketones or produces them on hydrolysis. It ranges from simpler monomer to large polymers.

**Give general representation of carbohydrates?**

**Ans**- In carbohydrates the ratio of C: H: O is 1:2:1 and can be represented by the stoichiometric formula **$(CH_2O)n$,** where n is the number of C in the molecule.

**Give biological importance of carbohydrates?**

**Ans**-1. Carbohydrates are important source of energy for metabolism.

2. Carbohydrates are important storage & structural materials in plants.

**Can human body survive without carbohydrates?**

**Ans**- Yes, body uses protein and fats for energy in absence of carbohydrate.

**Define monosachharides ?**

**Ans**- Simple sugars, which cannot be hydrolyzed further are known as monosaccharides. Based on number of carbon atoms monosaccharides further categorized as -

a. **Triose** – consist of 3 Carbon atoms - Glyceraldehyde & dihydroxyacetone.
b. **Tetrose** consist of 4 Carbon atoms - Erythrose.
c. **Pentose** -consist of 5 Carbon atoms. - ribose & deoxyribose sugar in nucleic acids.
d. **Hexose** consist of 6 Carbon atoms Glucose, fructose, Galactose, etc.

**Which carbohydrates are aldose & ketoses?**

**Ans**- Carbohydrates can also be classified on basis of functional groups. Those that posses aldehyde (CHO) as functional group are known as aldose, and those that posses carbonyl (C=O ) group as ketose. Ex- Glucose & fructose both are hexoses (6-C ) but Glucose is an aldohexose, whereas fructose is ketohexose.

**What are oligosaccharides?**

**Ans**- Oligosaccharides are made up of 2-10 monosaccharide. Depending on no of monosaccharide units, they are classified as disaccharides(2 monosaccharide units), triasaccharides (3units), and so on.

**Define disaccharides with suitable examples.**

**Ans**- Compounds that produce two monosaccharides on hydrolysis.

Example **Sucrose**= Glucose + fructose

**Maltose** = Glucose + Glucose

**Lactose** = Glucose + Galactose.

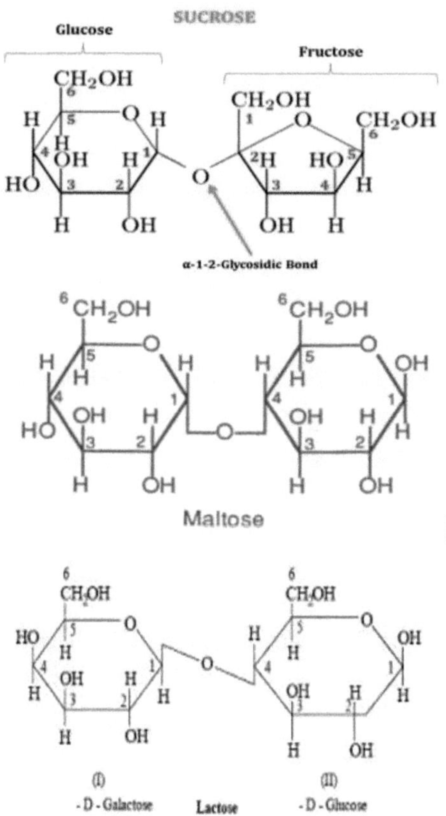


Sucrose Maltose Lactose

**What is milk sugar?**

**Ans-** Lactose is milk sugar ( β-D-Galactopyranosyl- (1-4 )-D-glucopyranose).

**What is lactose intolerance?**

**Ans-** Lactose intolerance is usually caused by a deficiency of an enzyme in the body called lactase.

**How does maltose hydrolysis ?**

**Ans**- Maltose is further hydrolyzed by the enzyme maltase to produce two molecules of D-glucose,It is linked by an α-(1,4′) glycosidic bond.

**What are sources of maltose?**

**Ans**- Maltose( α-D-Glucopyranosyl-(1-4) D-glucopyranose). It's a degradation product of starch. Malt is good source of it.

**How many stereoisomers are possible for glucose?**

**Ans**- The possible number of stereoisomers can be calculated by using formula **$X=2^n$**. where n is no of asymmetric carbon atom. Glucose ( aldohexose) contains 3 asymmetric carbon atom therefore have $2^4$=16 possible stereoisomers.

**What is ring or cyclic structure of monosaccahrides?**

**Ans**- Linear chain structure of monosaccharide do not explain some observation. Such as

1. Glucose like other aldehydes do not restore the colour of Fuschine decolourized by $SO_2$ (schiff's fuschine).

2. Mutarotation of freshly prepared glucose solution. Therefore Tollen proposed a structure where C-1 become asymmetric after appearance of cycle formed by elimination of $H_20$ between CHO group ( reacting in the form of aldehyde hydrate and OH at C-5 forming an oxide bridge.

**What is pyranose & furanose form?**

**Ans**- Pyranose is hexagonal whereas, furanose is pentagonal ring structure.

In case of Aldoses cyclization involve 1-5 oxide bridge (pyranose) and 1-4oxide bridge (furanose).

For ketoses (fructose) C-2( ketone group)form oxide bridge either to C-6 (pyranose) or carbon 5 ( furanose ring).

**What is epimers?**

**Ans**- Epimers are stereoisomers that differ (position at a single carbon atom) in the configuration of atoms attached to a chiral carbon. For example Glucose & Mannose are epimers at C-2, Glucose & Galactose are epimers at C-4.

D-Mannose
(epimer at C-2)

D-Glucose

D-Galactose
(epimer at C-4)

Epimers

**What are anomers?**

**Ans-** Anomers are cyclic monosaccharides or glycosides that are epimers, differing from each others in the configuration of C-1for aldoses or in the configuration at C-2 for ketoses.

Example α-D-glucose and β- D-glucose

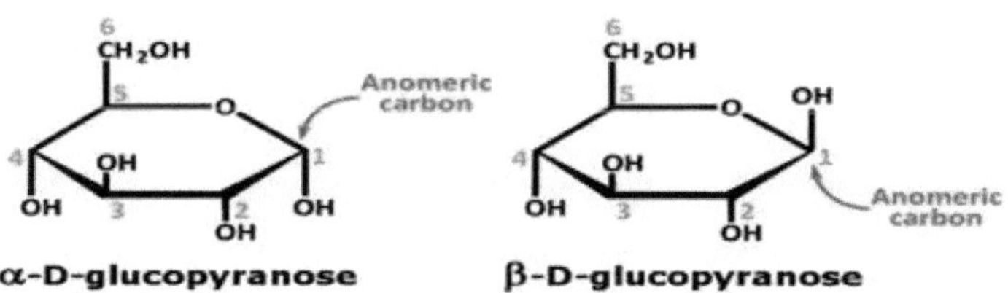


Anomers

**What is mutarotation?**

**Ans-** Mutarotation is the change in (equilibrium) specific rotation of a chiral compound due to epimerization.

**What is invert sugar?**

**Ans-** Hydrolysis of sucrose (specific rotation + $66.5^0$) produce a mixture of glucose (specific rotation + $52.5^0$) and fructose (specific rotation - $92^0$). Specific rotation of solution overall changes from positive to negative (invert).

**What is reducing sugar?**

**Ans-**Sugars with free aldehyde or ketone group are able to reduce metal ions under alkaline conditions are called as reducing sugars. (cupric ion to cuprous stat- fehling or benedict's solution). Ex- Glucose, galactose, lactose, maltose.

**Why smaltose is reducing sugar?**

**Ans-** Due to free aldehyde group, maltose is a reducing sugar and forms osazone with phenylhydrazine.

**How sucrose is non reducing sugar ?**

**Ans-** Sucrose is disaccharide consisting of glucose & fructose. Reducing group $C_1$ of α-glucose and $C_2$ of β-fructose involved in bond formation and not free to oxidized by a weak oxidizing agent in basic aqueous solution.

**Give systemic name of raffinose?**

**Ans-**β-D-Furctofuranosyl-O-α-D-galactopyranosyl-(1-6)-α-D-glucopyranose.

**What are sources of sucrose?**

**Ans-** sugar cane , sugar beet, etc.

**What is polysaccharide?**

**Ans-** High molecular weight carbohydrates, which on hydrolysis gives more than ten molecules of monosaccharide.

**What is homopolysaccharides?**

**Ans-** Polysaccharides, that contain only one type of monosaccharides (same repeating units). Ex-

a. **Starch** - polysaccharide of Glucose with α-(1,4) bond. It is storage polysaccharide in plant/ food. Abundantly found in plant roots, tuber, stem fruits.

b. **Glycogen** - polysaccharide of Glucose- α-(1,4) bond- It is main storage/reserve polysaccharide in animal also known as animal starch.Stored primarily in liver & muscles.
c. **Inulin**- storage polysaccharide in plant specifically composite family. Its polymer of fructose. (1-2 β linked)
d. **Cellulose** - polysaccharide of Glucose with β -(1-4) bond. It's a Structural Component (20-40 %) of plant cell wall. Cotton fibre is 90 % cellulose. Most abundant organic substance on earth.

**What is amylose & Amylopectin?**

**Ans**- Starch is large polymer consist of amylose & amylopectin. amylose- is soluble, unbranched, linear chain of glucose (α -1-4 linkage) of about 200-300 glucose residue. Whereas, amylopectin is branched, insoluble structure (α- 1-6 linkage).

**What is reason for formation of blue color when starch reacts with iodine?**

**Ans**- Iodine reacts with helices of linear chain (amylose) and gives blue colour. Amylopectin gives purple color with iodine.

**Which protein helps for initiation of glycogen synthesis in liver?**

**Ans**- Glycogenin – it acts as privation mer to initiates glucose polymerization for glycogen synthesis.

**What is structural polysaccharide?**

**Ans**- Polysaccharide that provide structural integrity or support. Example- **Murein**-Polysaccharide stabilize cell wall of bacteria its consists of alternating units of N-acetylglucosamine (GluNAC) & N-acetylmeuraminic acid (MurNAC) by β -1-4 bond.

**What is heterpolysaccharide ?**

**Ans**- Heteropolysacchrides consists of two or more alternately repeating units.

**What is hyluronic acid? Give its biological importance.**

**Ans**- It is a glycosaminoglycan. Its present in vitreous body of eyes (as it has very high capacity to bind water). In synovial fluids of joints it serves function of lubrication and shock absorber.

**How to identify carbohydrates?**

**Ans**- Identification of carbohydrates needs followings tests to performed.

**Molisch test**-In presence of strong acid (con. $H_2SO_4$) polysacchrides are converted to monosacchrides and and dehydrated to form furfural (in case of pentoses) and hydroxymethylfurfural derivatives (hexoses) that on reaction with α-napthol produce violet colored complex. This is general test for carbohydrate.

**Seliwanoff's test:** this is a specific test for ketohexoses. Concentrated hydrochloric acid dehydrates ketohexoses to form furfural derivatives which condense with resorcinol to give a cherry red complex. Appearance of red color indicates positive test.

**Rothera's test:** Nitroprosside in alkaline medium reacts with keto group of ketone bodies (acetone and acetoacetate) to form a purple ring.

The inhibition of glycolysis by oxygen is referred to as Pasteur effect. This is due to inhibition of the enzyme phosphofructokinase by ATP and citrate (formed in the presence of O2)

# II

# Protein

**What are amino acid ?**

**Ans-** Amino acids are organic acids. They posses amino group attached to α-carbon hence called α amino acid. Other atoms attached to chiral C are H, COOH & side chain alkyl group R(except Glycine).

**How many standard amino acid are there?**

**Ans-** There are 20 standard amino acids found in all protein.

**How amino acids are classified?**

**Ans-Aromatic amino acids-** Phenylalanine, Tyrosine, Tryptophan **Basic amino acids-** Arginine, Lysine, Histidine

**Acidic amino acid-** Aspartic acid and Glutamic acid

**Sulfur containing amino acids** -Cysteine, Methionine, Cystine (formed from 2 cysteine).

**Name the amino acid that devoid of asymmetric C atom.**

**Ans-** Glycine (posses $NH_2$, COOH, H & H) because of 2 H its central C atom is not asymmetric or chiral. It is simplest & smallest amino acid.

**What is zwitterions & isoionic pH?**

**Ans-** Compound which posses equal no of positive & negative charge, so that overall net charge posses by molecule is zero is known as zwitterions.

pH at which compounds exist as zwitter ion is called isoionic pH/ isoelectric pH.

Amino acids besides side chain R, have carboxyl & amino group. Addition of acid is (H+) following reaction occurs

$COO^- + H^+$---- $COOH$ & $NH_2 + H^+$ ------------ $NH_3$.

And when base added reverse reaction take place

$COOH$ ---- $COO^- + H^+$ & $NH_3$-------- $NH_2 + H^+$.

Charge on molecules depends on pH of solution. At isoionic pH net charge is 0. Below pI is negative and above pI has positive charge.

Eg. Alanine with pI =6.07

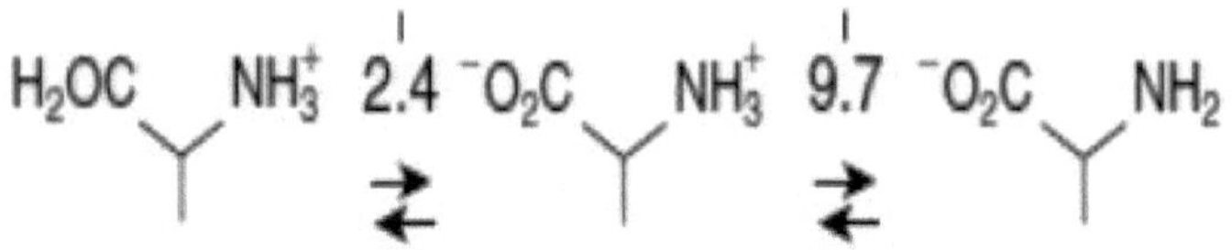

$H_2OC$ $NH_3^+$ 2.4 $^-O_2C$ $NH_3^+$ 9.7 $^-O_2C$ $NH_2$

Alanine with pI =6.07

**What is protein?**

**Ans-** Proteins are polymers of amino acids which are joined together by peptide bond(CO-NH).

**How many amino acids make up a protein? Which is 21st amino acid?**

**Ans-** 20 known standard amino acid make up proteins. Selenocysteineis 21st amino acid.

**What is the average molecular weight of an amino acid residue in a protein?**

**Ans-** 110 Da.

**What is naturally occurring form of amino acid in proteins?**

**Ans-** L- Amino acid (D – amino acid found in bacteria).

**What is nutritionally essential & non- essential amino acid?**

**Ans-**

Amino acids that are not synthesized in body & therefore require through diet are known as essential amino acids .Ex- Val, Leu, Ile, Met, Phy,Trp,Thr, Lys. Amino acids that are synthesized in body (from amphibolic intermediates or from other dietary amino acids) are known as non-essential. TCA intermediate α-ketoglutarate (Glu, Gln, Pro, Hyp), Oxaloacetate ( Asp,Asn), Glycolytic intermediate3-phosphoglycerate(Ser & Gly), (Cys, Tyr,Hyl) formed from other essential amino acid.

| Non-essential | Essential | 'Conditionally' essential |
| --- | --- | --- |
| alanine | valine | cysteine |
| serine | leucine | tyrosine |
| asparagine | isoleucine | glutamine |
| aspartate | methionine | arginine |
| glutamate | phenylalanine | proline |
| | threonine | glycine |
| | lysine | taurine |
| | histidine | |
| | tryptophan | |

**Essential & non- essential amino acid**

Amino acids that are not synthesized in body & therefore require through diet are known as essential amino acids .Ex- Val, Leu, Ile, Met, Phy,Trp,Thr, Lys. Amino acids that are synthesized in body (from amphibolic intermediates or from other dietary amino acids) are known as non-essential. TCA intermediate α-ketoglutarate (Glu, Gln, Pro, Hyp), Oxaloacetate ( Asp,Asn), Glycolytic intermediate3-phosphoglycerate(Ser & Gly), (Cys, Tyr,Hyl) formed from other essential amino acid.

**Which Diseases is caused by protein deficiency?**

**Ans-** Kwashiorkor.

**What is monomeric and oligomeric protein?**

**Ans-** Protein made up of single polypeptide is known as monomeric. If it contains two or more polypeptides, then its known as oligomeric protein. For example Human Insulin (53 AA) is dimericas it consists of two polypeptide chain A (22 AA) & B (33AA). Haemoglobin, Hb is tetramer with 4 polypeptide chains (2 identical α & 2 identical-β).

**What is (primary) 1° structure of proteins?**

**Ans-** Number & sequence of amino acid residues joined by peptide bonds constitute primary structure.

Determination of primary structure involves fragmentation of protein using site specific enzyme or chemicals, Sequencing of fragments, determing N & C terminals, overlapping fragments, etc.

**What is secondary structure? Name the most common secondary structure.**

**Ans-** Right handed α Helix ismost common secondary structure. In α helix single polypeptide chain is coiled spirally by establishing hydrogen bond between $1^{st}$ and $4^{th}$ amino acid residue. Each turn contains 3.6 Amino acid residue have pitch of 0.54nm. Left handed α-helix though energetically possible, are of rare occurrence.

β -sheets, - is stretched conformation of protein, produced by holding two or more polypeptide chains by means of hydrogen bonds. Two polypeptides running in same direction (parallel β sheets) or if run in opposite direction (antiparallel β-sheet)

β turns- It consists of 4 amino acid residues arranged in such a fashion that polypeptide moves in opposite direction (reverse about 180°).

**What is tertiary structure of protein? Name the forces that stabilize this structure.**

**Ans-** Three-dimensional folding of polypeptide chain is known tertiary structure. Hydrogen bond, Hydrophobic interactions, Ionic interactions, Van den walls forces stabilize the 3-D structure(week non-covalent) interactions.

**What is responsible to specify the three-dimensional shape of a protein?**

**Ans**- The protein's amino acid sequence (primary structure) is ultimately responsible for it.

**Name the protein that sequenced first?**

**Ans**- Insulin, sequenced by Frederick Sanger.

**Which food products are high in protein content?**

**Ans**- Tofu and eggs, Grains and legumes, Milk and milk products.

**What is protein denaturation / coagulation?**

**Ans**- Destabilization of 3-D structure results in loss of biological activity of protein is known as protein denaturation and agents responsible for this is known as denaturating agents.

**Name the factor responsible for protein denaturation?**

**Ans**- High temperature, extreme of pH, high energy radiations, chemical agents such as alcohol urea, salts of heavy metals responsible for this.

**What is quaternary structure of protein? Give example.**

**Ans**- Association of two or more polypeptides to form protein is known as quaternary structure. For example Hb ( protein binds $O_2$) posses quaternary structure- total 4 polypetides (2α & 2β chain).

**How are protein classified on the basis of shape?**

**Ans**- a. Firbous- also known as scelro-proteins protein-ex, elastin, collagen, actin, myosin, keratin

b. Globular – Hb, histones ( protein associated with DNA), egg albumin, serum globulin, etc.

**How are the protein classified on basis of complexity?**

**Ans**-

a. Simple preotein- eg. glutenin of wheat, oryzenin, zeatin-storage protein.
b. Conjugated protein- conjugated with additional group- eg. Nucleoprotein ( with nucleic acids), chromoprotein -flavoproteins (with FMN/ FAD), cytochrome & hemocyanin, chloroplastin with chlorophyll, Lipoprotein – with lipid (Lipovetellin of egg yolk), Phosphoprotein- ( phosphate) casein-milk protein. Glycoprotein or mucoprotein-mucin of saliva
c. Derived protein-Terpenes, Steroids etc.

**Ceruloplasmin protein carries which metal?**

**Ans-** Copper.

**What is Ramachandran plot?**

**Ans-** It give idea regarding combination of Pi (rotation about N-$C_\alpha$) & psi (rotation about $C_\alpha$ –C.) angles.

**What is renaturation of proteins?**

**Ans-** Conversion of denatured protein to its native form is known as renaturation. Enzyme ribonuclease, with 124 amino acids and 4disulfide bonds when treated with beta mercaptoethanol & urea leads to denaturation (formation of 8 –SH sites ).On Removal of these chemical agents disulfide bonds restore spontaneously generating active enzyme.

**What is biological role of protein?**

**Ans-** Besides growth & repair protein perform following task.

1) Important constituents of cell /plasma membrane

2) As enzyme- allow all metabolic reaction to take place

3) As hormones (Insulin, Gowth hormone, glucagon, etc)

4) Structural elements provide shape & stability.

a. Keratin present in nails, claws, horns, hairs Wool- Large of keratin contain right handed α-helix , 2 chain form left hand supercoiling, This dimerize, tetramerize then form protofilament (3nm), eight protofilament join to form 10nm intermediate filament.

b. Elastin – in ligaments and tubulin in microtubule.

c. Collagen in tendons & cartilage & connective tissue- important protein about 25% of total protein.Collagentriple helixconsists of three collagen helices. Triplet of Gly-X-Yis of frequently repeated in the sequence of collagen, (X position occupied by Pro and Y by Hyp)

d. Fibroin- silk protein produce by silkworm. Consists of $\beta_\alpha$ sheet structure & repetitive amino acid sequence (Gly-Ala-Gly-Ala-Gly-Ser). pleated sheet layers in fibroin are found to lie alternately 0.35 nm and 0.57 nm apart.

5) Carrier or transport protein- Hb- $O_2$

6) Defense/ protection – Immunoglobulin Ig.

**What are different methods for estimation of proteins?**

**Ans-** Micro –Kjeldahl method -used for total or crude protein estimation. Method of choice for food material, agriculture samples.

**Biuret method-** Not highly accurate but fast method for protein determination (range 0.5-5mg). It works on principle that peptide bond of protein form purple complex with copper ion in alkaline condition. ( 520 nm reading).

Lowry's method- Protein reacts with FCR Folin Ciocalteu reagent to form blue colour complex. The color formed is because of reaction of alkaline copper as with biuret & the reduction of Phosphomolybdate & tungustate in FCR by tyrosine & tryptophan in protein, therefore intensity is dependent on amount of these aromatic amino acid present. This is 10 times sensitive than biuret. (read at 660 nm).

UV- absorption $E_{280}$nm- Most proteins have maximum absorption at 280 nm due to aromatic amino acids. This works well with pure solution.

Bradford's method- dye binding method for soluble protein.

# III

# Lipid

**What is lipid?**

**Ans-** Lipid is term used to describe class of compounds that is of biological origin and soluble in organic solvents ( ex.methanol, alcohol, benzene) but insoluble or only sparingly soluble in aqueous solution.

**What is biological role of Lipids?**

**Ans-** 1. As a fuel for metabolic energy- Adipocytes stores a lipid (neutral fats) and release fatty acids whenever needed.

2. Important structural constituent of plasma membrane

3. Insulator- Deposition of lipids around organs and tissues provides mechanical & thermal insulation. (regulate body temperature preventing heat loss)

4. Waterproof coating on leaves, fruits.

4. Hormones, vitamins & signaling molecules - (sterols, eicosanoids , etc).

**What are saturated fatty acids (SFA)?**

**Ans-** A Saturated fatty acid is a type of fat in which the fatty acid chains have all single bonds.

**Give examples of saturated Fatty acid.**

**Ans-**

Caproic acid- **HOOC-$(CH_2)_4$--CH3** (6:0)

Caprilyc acid- **HOOC-$(CH_2)_6$-CH3** (8:0)

Capric acid - **HOOC--$(CH_2)_8$-CH3** (10:0)
Lauric acid - **HOOC--$(CH_2)_{10}$-CH3** (12:0)
Myristic acid- **HOOC--$(CH_2)_{12}$--CH3** (14:0)
Palmitic acid - **HOOC--$(CH_2)_{14}$--CH3** (16:0)
Stearic acid - **HOOC--$(CH_2)_{16}$-CH3** (18:0)
Arachidic acid **HOOC--$(CH_2)_{18}$-CH3** (20:0)
Behenic acid- **HOOC--$(CH_2)_{20}$-CH3** (22:0)
Lignoceric acid- **HOOC--$(CH_2)_{22}$-CH3** (24:0)

**What is unsaturated fatty acid (UFA)?**

**Ans-** Unsaturated fatty acids have one or more carbon – Carbon double bonds.

**What isMUFA?**

**Ans-** MUFA stands for monounsaturated fatty acids. Fatty acids that contains single double bond.

Example- Palmitoleic acid (16:1,9)
HOOC-$(CH_2)_7$ -CH=CH-$(CH_2)_5$ -$CH_3$
Oleic acid (18:1,9)
HOOC-$(CH_2)_7$ -CH=CH-$(CH_2)_7$ -$CH_3$

**What isPUFA** ?

**Ans-** PUFA stands for polyunsaturated fatty acids. Fatty acids contains 2 or more C-C double bonds.

Example- Linoleic acid 18:2, 9,12
HOOC-$(CH_2)_7$ -CH=CH-$CH_2$-CH=CH-$(CH_2)_4$ -$CH_3$
Linolenic acid (18:3 9,12,15)
HOOC-$(CH_2)_7$ -CH=CH-$CH_2$-CH=CH- $CH_2$-CH=CH -$CH_2$-$CH_3$
Archidonic acid (20:4 5,8,11,14)
COOH-$(CH2)_3$-CH=CH-$CH_2$-CH=CH-$CH_2$.CH=CH-$CH_2$-CH=CH-$(CH_2)_4$-$CH_3$

**What is essential fatty acid?**

**Ans-** Fatty acids that are not synthesized in body and has to supplied in diet are known as essential fatty acid.

Examples-Linoleic acid (18:2; 9,12) and Linolenic acid (18:3 9,12,15 ).

**What is system for nomenclature of fatty acids?**

**Ans**- Numbering – it starts from COOH group which numbered as C-1

Greek letters- Such as α, β, and so on to number carbon atom and starts form α-to represent carbon next to carboxylic group COOH ($C_2$).

ω (omega) system- In this system the most distant carbon ($CH_3$) from COOH group designated as 1. Example-Linolenic acid having double bond between last 3rd & 4th Carbon atom is known as ω -3 fatty acid & Linoleic acid as ω-6 fatty acid.

**Which factors decides the melting point of fats?**

**Ans**- a. length of the fatty acid residues – shorter the fatty acid residue –lower the melting point.

b. number of their double bonds- more the numbers of double bonds, lower the melting point.

**What is rancidity?**

**Ans**- Unpleasant taste and odour which develops spontaneously in fats is known as rancidity. Small amount of free fatty acid (FFA) is present in oil which increases with storage. Reason for this is hydrolytic rancidity that results, due to hydrolysis of triglycerides into free fatty acid FFA & glycerol by microbe's (grow during storage period) lipases. Other is oxidative rancidity- oxidation of double bond of fatty acid in presence $O_2$ to form aldehydes, ketones & fatty acids with low mol wt (butyric, caproic acid) leading to unpleasantness.

**Define acid no & mention its significance?**

**Ans**- Its defined as mg of KOH (potassium hydroxide) required to neutralize the free fatty acid present in 1g of sample. Acid no therefore gives idea regarding FFA and therefore age and quality of oil or fat.

**What is peroxide number?**

**Ans**- It's a measure of peroxide contained in the oil and is determined by titration against thiosulfate in presence of KI with starch indicator.

**What is iodine value?**

**Ans**- It is a measure of degree of unsaturation of fat/oil and its characteristic of particular oil or fat. Halogen, (ICl) iodine chloride, reacts with double bond of unsaturated fat. Remaining iodine determined by titration with thiosulfate, this gives idea about iodine utilized and consequently the degree of unsaturation in given oil or fats.

**What is saponification and saponification number ?**

**Ans**- Fat or oil (triglycerides) when heated with (alkali) KOH forms potassium salts of fatty acids (soaps) and glycerol . Saponification value is defined as the number of mg of KOH required to saponify the fatty acids resulting from complete hydrolysis of 1g of fat/oil. The longer the carbon chain, the less acid is liberated per gram of fat hydrolysed. Therefore this number gives idea regarding nature of fatty acid chain length present in given sample.

**Give the classification of lipid?**

**Ans**- Lipids classified as simple lipid or compound lipids.

Simple lipid- are alcohol esters of fatty acids.

a. Nuetral fats- Esterification of glycerol with three molecules of fatty acids forms triacylglerols or triglyceride. It is also known as neutral fats since dosen't carry any charge. It acculmulate in adipose tissue.
b. Waxes – ester of fatty acid with alcohol other than glycerol. Ex. Bee wax

Complex lipids - consists of phospholipid, glycolipid/ sphingolipid, steroids,

Derived lipids- lipid soluble vitamins, hormones, fatty aldehydes

.

**What is phospholipid?**

**Ans**- Group of compounds characterized by two fatty acids attached to glycerol. Third OH group of glycerol is esterified to phosphoric acid. This phosphate in turn bound to second alcohol molecule which can be choline,ethanolamine, inositol, serine.

**Why phospholipids are said to be amphiphatic molecules?**

**Ans**- As Phosholipids contains long hydrophobic tail (2 fatty acids) & hydrophilic head (phosphate) it's said to be amphiphatic.

**Give one importance of phospholipid.**

**Ans**- Phospholipids are the essential components of all cell membranes.

**Give different classes of phospholipids. What is phosphatidate?**

**Ans**- Presence of phosphate group at C-3 of glycerols with two different fatty acyl residue attached to C-1 and C-2 (phosphatidate).

**Give different classes of phospholipid?**

**Ans**- a. Phosphatidylcholine - PC : When Phosphate group of phosphatidate esterified with OH group of amino alcohol choline $HOCH_2CH_2N\text{-}^+(CH_3)$ 3, produces PC . It's also known as lecithin. It's abundant membrane Phospholipid.

b. Phosphatidylethanolamine-PEWhen Phosphate group of phosphatidate esterified with OH group of amino alcohol ethanolamine ($HOCH_2CH_2NH_3^+$) produce PE also known as cephalin.

c. Phosphatidylserine PS- When Phosphate group of phosphatidate esterified with OH group serine produces PS.

Phosphatidylinositol- When Phosphate group of phosphatidate esterified with OH group sugar alcohol myo-inositol produce Phosphatidylinositol.

**What are sphingolipids?**

**Ans**- Glycerol is replaced by sphingosine, an amino alcohol with an unsaturated alkyl side chain, when sphingosine forms an amide bond to a fatty acid, the compound is called ceramide.

**What are cerebroside?**

**Ans**- Cerebroside is characterized by presence of galactose or glucose in molecule, and is important for the animal muscles, brain and nerve cell membranes.

**What cerebrosides contains?**

**Ans**- They consist of ceramide with a single sugar residue at one-hydroxyl moiety.

**What is the function of cerebrosides?**

**Ans-** It is essential for lamellar body in the stratum corneum to maintain the water permeability barrier of the skin.

**What is ganglioside?**

**Ans-** Ganglioside is a complex molecule composed of Sphingosine, fatty acids, carbohydrates( Lactose + galactosamine) and neuraminic acid. These are polar molecules.

**Where are the gangliosides found?**

**Ans-** Body fluids, tissues, nervous system, in cells primarily localized in the outer leaflets of plasma membranes.

**What is the function of gangliosides?**

**Ans-** Function as specific determinants in cellular recognition and cell-cell communication.

**What are proteolipids?**

**Ans-** Proteolipid, is a protein covalently linked to lipid molecules, which can be fatty acids or sterols.

**What are steroids?**

**Ans-** A steroid is a lipid derived from complex ring structure (cyclopentanoperhydrophenanthrine)nucleus (four ring arranged in a specific molecular configuration). Ex- Cholesterol. Estrogen , progesterone, vit A. ergosterol in plants.

**What are sources of cholesterol?**

**Ans-** Foodsuff such as butter, egg yolk, meat, liver, and brain are rich sources of cholesterol.

**How many carbon atoms are present in steroids structure?**

**Ans-** There is seventeen carbon atoms are present in steroids structure.

**What is basic unit for synthesis of steroids?**

**Ans-** Activated Isoprene unit (2-methyl-1,3-butadiene) is building block for steroids through, geraniol, farnesol, squalene.

**What do you mean by prostaglandin?**

**Ans-** Prostaglandins are a group of physiologically active lipid compound called eicosanoid having diverse hormone- like effect in animals.

**What is Bile &where it is stored.**

**Ans-** Bile is a greenish-yellow fluid made by liver and stored in our gallbladder.

**Give examples of bile salts & how it help in fat digestion?**

**Ans-** Potasium taurocholate and sodium glycocholate are bile salts and helps in the emulsification of fats.

# IV

# Nucleic acid

**What is nucleic acid?**

**Ans-** Nucleic acid is Polynucleotide strand i.e., polymer of several nucleotides, with adjacent nucleotides joined by 3'-5' phosphodiester bond. Ex-DNA (double stranded ) & RNA (single stranded).

**Why it's known as nucleic acid?**

**Ans-** It is acidic in nature and isolated from nucleus of pus cell so named as nucleic acid friedrich Meischer in 1868.

**What is biological significance of nucleic acid?**

**Ans-** Storage & transmission of genetic information (DNA).

Expression of genetic information or translation (RNA)

Cyclic nucleotides acts as messenger/ signal in metabolism.

**What isnucleoside?**

**Ans-** Nitrogenous base + pentose sugar.

**What is the composition ofnucleotide**?

**Ans-** Nitrogenous base + pentose sugar + phosphate. Pentose sugar is ribose in RNA & deoxyribose (at C-2 )in DNA. C-1 of sugar form *N*-glycosidic(β) bond with N-9 of purine or N-1 of pyrimidine.

**Give classification of nitrogenous bases in nucleic acid**.

**Ans-** Nitogenous basesare classified as purines & pyrimidines. Purines are double ring compounds and two purines bases includes Adenine (A), Guanine (G). Pyrimidines- are single ring compounds and contains Cytosine (C), Thymine (T), Uracil (U in RNA instead of T).

**What is Chargaff's rule?**

**Ans-** In 1950 Chargaff's come out with certain findings about DNA called Chargaff's rule. These are-

a. Purines & pyrimidines occur in equal amount.
b. Equal number of phosphate & deoxy-ribose sugar.
c. Molar amount of Adenine is equal to Thymine and Cytosine to Guanine.
d. A+T/C+G ratio is species specific & Its rarely one.

**Give the no of hydrogen bonds between purine & pyrimidines.**

**Ans-** Adenine of one strand paired with Thymine of other strand with two hydrogen bond, while Cytosine & Thymineform three hydrogen bonds.

**Which ratio is constant for DNA?**

**Ans-** A + G / T + C

**Arrangement of nucleotides in DNA can be seen by.**

**Ans-** X-Ray crystallography.

**Name the scientist who received noble prize for structure of DNA.**

**Ans-** Watson, Crick & Wilkins.

**Describe the structure of DNA.**

**Ans-** Watson & Crick give model of DNA in 1953 known as B-DNA. It is consisting of two antiparallel polydeoxyribonucleotide strands helically coiled with each other around a common central axis. Backbone of strand is produced by alternate sugar and phosphate. Two strands held together by Hydrogen bonding between complementary nitrogen bases, purine of one strands pairs with pyrimidines of other to form base pair (A -T & C-G) DNA helix has diameter of 20 $A^0$, and each turn of helix contain 10 base pairs (10.5 BP). Plane of base is perpendicular to central axis. Alternate major and minor grooves observed throughout DNA length due to coiling of two strands around each other.

**What is base stacking?**

**Ans-** Arrangement of bases in DNA helix results in piling up of base pairs one above other (similar to pile of coins) this is known as base stacking. Base stacking provides additional stability to structure of DNA besides base pairing.

**What is handedness of A DNA?**

**Ans-** Both A & B DNA is right-handed. A DNAis broadest and has 11 base pairs /turn, with glycosidic bond in anti conformation. Dehydration of B DNA induces formation of A DNA.

Which nucleic acids posses a left-handed Helix?

Ans- Z-DNA ( Z stands for zig-zag appearance of phosphate groups along the backbone ). It is narrow in shape with 12 base pair/ turn and diameter of about 18 $A^0$, glycosidic bond with alternate anti and syn conformation. Z DNA observed in region of short stretches of DNA where purines alternates pyrimidines.

**What is DNA denaturation & how it is measured?**

**Ans-** Unwinding or separation of two strands is known as DNA denaturation or meltingand can be studied by measuring increase in absorbance at 260 nm (as exposed aromatic bases in single stranded DNA absorb more compared to double stranded DNA, this is known as Hyperchromicity).

# V

# Vitamins

**What are vitamins?**

**Ans**- Vitamins are essential organic compounds, with specific biological activity, which are required in small amount in diet.

**Who coined the term vitamin?**

**Ans**- Funk .

**Name the water soluble & Fat soluble vitamins.**

**Ans-Water soluble**-vitamin-B complex & vitamin C,

**Fat soluble vitamins** – A, D, E, K

**What is vitamin A & give its functions.**

**Ans**- Vitamin A is retinol. Its aldehyde form retinal present in rod cells of retina (rhodopsin protein), It form part of visual pigments, prevents keratinization of epithelia, growth. Daily need in adults is about 2mg. Present in animal cod liver oil, In plants- (found in pro-vitamin form) green leafy vegetables, carrot (B- carotene), milk butter, etc. Vitamin A is destroyed by strong light.

**What are deficiency symptoms of Vitamin A?**

**Ans**- Night blindness (inability to see in dim light), xerophthalmia (dryness of conjunctiva), Keratinization of epithelia.

**What is vitamin B?**

**Ans**- Vitamin B is a complex of several vitamins: riboflavin, folate, nicotinate, and pantothenic acid.

**What is Vitamin B1? Give its functions.**

**Ans**- Vitamin B1 also called as Thiamine, its daily requirement in adult is about 1.5mg. Peanuts, beans, lean meat are common sources of it. Function as part of coenzymes (TPP- Thymine pyrophosphate) for carbohydrate metabolism, pentose synthesis etc. Its destroyed by baking soda.

**What is Beri-beri disease?**

**Ans**- Deficiency of thiamine/ Vitamin B1 lead to beri-beri. Dry beri beri-a condition characterized by wasting of muscules, apetite loss- Wet beri- beri- heart failure. It occurs in outer layer of grains such as cereals, legumes, etc. Eating of polished rice & use of refined flour also lead to beri-beri, as the vitamin is removed during these processes.

**What are the sources & function of vitamin $B_2$?**

**Ans**- Vitamin B-2 also known as Riboflavin. As part of coenzyme it exists in two form FMN (fllavin-monomucleotide) & FAD (flavin-dinucleotide). Bright light destroy it. Its deficiency leads to eye damage, dermatitis of the face, Fissures at corners of mouth.

**Sources**- yeast, leafy vegetables, milk, cheese, intestinal bacteria are some of the common sources of Vitamin $B_2$, with daily need of about 2 mg. It forms a part of coenzyme.

**What are sources for Folic acid?**

**Ans**- Folic acid is found mostly in dark green vegetables like broccoli and spinach, legumes such as beans and peas, and enriched grains.

**What is active form of folic acid?**

**Ans**- Tetrahydrofolic acid ($TH_4$).

**What is function & sources of Niacin?**

**Ans**- Niacinor nicotinic acid has daily requirement of 20 mg /day. It is required for biosynthesis of two coenzymes nicotinamide adenine dinucleotide ($NAD^+$) and nicotinamide adenine dinucleotide phosphate ($NADP^+$)that brings about oxidation-reduction reactions. Peanuts, legumes, fish, cereals are sources of it.

**What is effect of deficiency of Niacin?**

**Ans**- Niacin deficiency causes pellagra, a disease characterized by skin lesions (scaly skin sores), gastrointestinal disorders (diarrhea), and mental disorders (mental confusion and hallucinations).

Pellagra observed in population that uses maize or jowar as main cereal.

**Describe the pyridoxine & mention its sources.**

**Ans-** Pyridoxine (pyridoxal & pyridoxamine) isvitamin $B_6$. Active form is PLPpyridoxal phoshphate - assist in amino acid metabolism (transamination) & glycogen synthesis & Pyridoxamine phosphate in decarboxylation of Amino acids. About 2 mg needed in adults daily. Egg yolk, Meat, milk, liver, banana etc. are good source of it. Cooking destroy it. Deficiency of this vitamins results in anemia, weight loss, skin lesions, CNS disorders.

**Vitamin $B_{12}$ (Cobalamine) is only synthesized by?**

**Ans-** Microorganism.

**Lack of which vitamin results in Anaemia (weakness)?**

**Ans-** Either a lack of vitamin $B_{12}$ or a lack of folate causes a type of anemia called megaloblastic anemia (enlargement of RBC).

**The hemorrhagic disease in newborn is caused due to deficiency of which vitamin?**

**Ans-** Vitamin K .

**What is the chemical name of vitamin B5 ?**

**Ans-** Vitamin $\mathbf{B_5}$ is Pantothenic acid required in Co-A & ACP Synthesis.

**What is chemical name of vitamin C?**

**Ans-** Vit C also known as ascorbic acid or ascorbate.

**Which vitamin deficiency leads to scurvy?**

**Ans-** Vitamin C required in formation for hydroxylation of Pro & lys residues in collagen, a cementing material/tissue formation. Deficiency of vitamin C therefore results into scurvy -loose teeth, swollen joints, delayed wound healing, osteoporosis & decreased immune-competence. Ascorbate also involved in iron metabolism.

**Give the sources of vitamin C.**

**Ans-** Fresh citrus fruit, aamla, berries-abundant source of vitamin C.

**What is vitamin D?**

**Ans-** Also known as calciferol, existed in 2 form ergocalciferol (vit D2) found in plants and cholecalciferol(D-3) found in animals. Active form of D3 is calcitrol (1,25 dihydroxycholecalciferol involved in calcification of bone, intestinal calcium absorption.

**Calcium deficiency in the body occurs in the absence of which vitamin?**

**Ans-** Vitamin D (calciferol).

**What is cheapest & richest source of vitamin D?**

**Ans-** Sunlight is the cheapest source-vitamin D is formed in skin from 7-dehydrocholesterol by action of by UV light. Others dietary sources includes, fish liver oil, egg, yolk.

**What does deficiency of vitamin D causes**?

**Ans-** Rickets in children and osteomalacia in adults.

**What is vitamin E? Give its functions.**

**Ans-** Vitamin E also known as tocopherol or α -tocopherol. Present in green leafy vegetable & vegetable oil. Vitamin E acts as antioxidants. Deficiency results in, destruction of erythrocytes, muscular dystrophy.

**What is role of vitamin K?**

**Ans-** Vitamin K is known as Phyllloquinone, required in trace amount 0.07-0.15mg. It helps in Blood clotting (synthesis of prothombin). Sources of its includes, soyabean, intestinal bacteria.

# VI

# Enzyme

**What are enzyme? How it differs from chemical catalyst?**

**Ans-** Enzymes are biological catalyst. Organic nature (protein), specificity ( catalyze specific reaction), catalytic efficiency (rate is high), regulation ( can be control) are characteristic of enzyme that differs it from chemical catalyst.

**Who discovered the first enzyme?**

**Ans-** Anselme payen .

**Who coined the term enzymes?**

**Ans-** William Kuhne.

**What is nature of enzymes?**

**Ans-** Protein in nature (except –Ribozyme – where RNA acts as enzyme catalyst).

**Name the enzyme that hydrolyze fat/oil.**

**Ans-** An enzyme called lipase catalyses the hydrolysis of the fats and oils.

**Define activation energy.**

**Ans-** Amount of energy required to reach transition state. It is equals to difference between the energy levels of the transition state and ground state.

**What are holoenzymes ?**

**Ans-** Catalytically active enzymes having both protein part (apoenzyme) and non-protein part (co-enzyme and or co factor is termed as holoenzymes.

**What are prosthetic group ?**

**Ans**- The enzymes bind cofactor more tightly which is difficult to remove called prosthetic group.

**Define turnover number.**

**Ans**- Number of substance molecules transformed per minute by a single enzyme molecule or by a single active site.

**What is katal?**

**Ans**- Katal is a amount of enzyme activity that transforms a mole of substrate per second (SI unit).

**What are zymogens or proenzymes?**

**Ans**- Inactive precursors of Enzymes are known as zymogens. Many proteolytic enzymes are biosynthesized as larger inactive precursors For example Trypsin- Trypsinogen, pepsin-pepsinogen.

**What are coenzymes**?

**Ans**- These are organic molecules binds with enzymes to assist in catalysis. Coenzymes are derivatives of vitamins.

**What is multienzyme system?**

**Ans**- When several enzymes work sequentially together in system (to form ultimate end product of pathway).

**Define Isoenzyme.**

**Ans**- These are similar forms, for the same enzyme catalyzing the same reactions. But have small differences in structure (one or few amino acids residues), or identical function but different structure.

**What is Allosteric enzyme?**

**Ans**- Enzymes possesses other site (known as Allostearic site) in addition to active site known as allosteric enzyme. Allosteric Inhibitorsbinds with allosteric site and prevents substrate binding at active site. Whereas activators after binding works oppositely.

**Who proposed Lock and key model of enzyme action?**

**Ans**- E.fisher 1894 explain about Rigidity and specificity(**complementarity**) between active site of E and S. Lock & Key anology with Enzyme & substrate.

**Name the fastest enzyme.**

**Ans**- Carbonic anhydrase ($CO_2$+$H_2O$ ----$H_2CO_3$---H + $HCO_3$) highest turnover is one of the fastest enzymes known ($10^6$ substrate converted to product/second).

**What is the optimum pH? Give examples.**

**Ans**- pH at which enzyme show it's maximum activity is known as optimum_pH. Example all protein degrading enzymes have different optimum pH of (Pepsin- 2, Trypsin- 8, Amylase- 6.8- 6.9).

**Define cofactor.**

**Ans**- Non-protein component (metal ions) without which the enzyme protein is inactive / slow.

**Name some enzymes that are active even at 100°C.**

**Ans**- Venom phosphokinases & muscle adenylate kinase.

**Name some cardiac enzymes.**

**Ans**- LDH (lactate dehydrogenase), CK (creatine kinase ), AST ( Aspartate transaminase) .

**Which model explains the flexibility of active site?**

**Ans**- Daniel koshland's Induced fit model 1958 . According to this, proximity of substrate induces slight conformational change (flexibility) in active site of enzyme to bind with substrate and form final complex ES, ultimately leading to formation of product and free enzyme.

**Name the enzyme secreted by kidney and regulates blood pressure.**

**Ans**- Renin .

**Name Enzyme that disrupts the bacterial cell wall.**

**Ans**- Lysozyme.

**Can enzyme be crystallized?**

**Ans**- Yes, first enzyme crystallized by James B Sumnerin 1926 is urease isolate from jack bean meal.

**What is enzyme inhibition?**

**Ans**- An enzyme inhibitor is a molecule that binds to an enzyme and decreases or stops its activity.

**What is competitive inhibition?**

**Ans**- An inhibitor, generally a substrate analogue binds to the enzyme, usually at the active site, and prevents the original substrate from binding. (Km change, Vmax remains same).

**What is EC no?**

**Ans-** Its Enzyme Commission number. Four digit code assigned to individual enzyme. First digit indicates class, second sub-class, third sub-sub-class, fourth individual enzyme in sub-sub-class. Its unique for each Enzyme.

**Give the six classes of enzyme.**

**Ans-** O,T,H,L,I,L .

1) oxido-reductases -These enzymes bring about oxidation and reduction. Ex- Alcohol dehydrogenase (EC No- 1.1.1.1)

2) Transferase - responsible for transferring functional groups from one molecule to another.

Ex- Aspartate amino transferase (EC No -2.6.1.1)

3) Hydrolases - catalyze reactions that involve hydrolysis. They break single bonds by adding water. Ex- alpha Amylase (EC No-3.2.1.1)

4) Lyases -catalyze reactions where functional groups are added to break double bonds in molecules or where double bonds are formed by the removal of functional groups.

Ex- Aldolase (EC No- 4.1.2.13)

5)Isomerases - catalyze the reactions where a functional group ismoved to another position within the same molecule (internal rearrangements) such that the resulting molecule is actually an isomer of the earlier molecule.

Ex- phosphotrioisomerase(EC-5.3.1.1)

6) Ligases -form bonds by removal of the water component.

Ex - glutamine synthetase (EC- 6.3.1.2)

**Identify the figure**

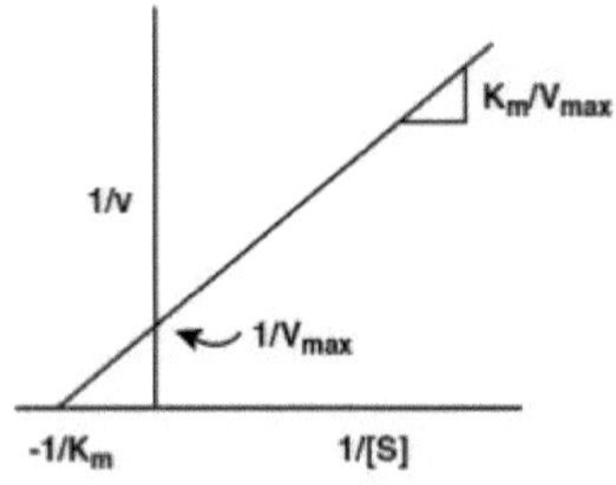


LB Plot

**Ans-** Its LB Plot

**Identify the figure**

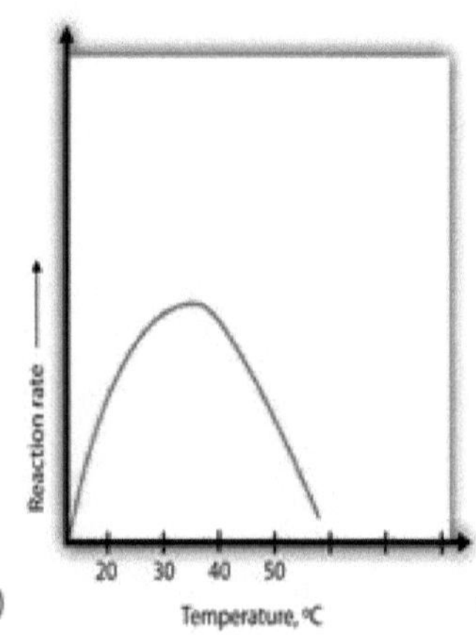

Effect of temperature on enzyme velocity

**Ans-** Effect of temperature on enzyme velocity
**Identify the figure**

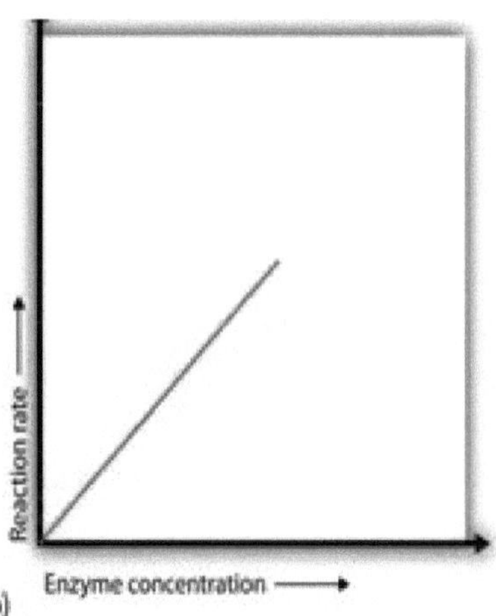


Effect of enzyme concentration on enzyme velocity

**Ans-** Effect of enzyme concentration on enzyme velocity
**What is Temperature coefficient?**
**Ans-** Increase in enzyme velocity when temperature is increased by 10 degree.
**The substrate binds at which site of enzyme**
**Ans-** Active site.

# VII
# Blood

**What is blood?**

**Ans**- Blood is fluid flowing connective tissue.

**What are Functions of blood?**

**Ans**- Transport of gases ($O_2$, $CO_2$), exchange of nutrients to tissues and collection of metabolic waste from tissues.

Homeostasis- Maintain internal environment (acid base balance by liver & kidney & body temperature etc)

Defense / protection- blood cells & proteins provides specific and non-specific defense against pathogens. (plasma proteins).

Self protection by blood clotting.

Distribution of Chemical signal/ hormones

**What is plasma?**

**Ans**- Liquid portion of blood is called plasma; it consists of cells (RBC-erythrocytes, WBC- leukocytes, and patelets- thrombocytes), various proteins, diffused gases, clotting factors (including fibrinogen),nutrients, etc. Included in category of Leukocytes are granulocytes (acidophils, basophils & neutrophils), monocyte (later develop into macrophages- a phagocytic cells), & lymphocytes (B & T lymocytes)

**What is serum?**

**Ans**- When blood comes out of body allowed to clot and subjected to centrifugation, results into straw, yellow colored liquid called serum (devoid of clotting factor fibrinogen as it is utilized in clot formation).

**Give details of plasma protein.**

**Ans**- Plasma proteins constitutes important part of plasma mainly synthesized by liver ( except- Antibodies and and divided into Albumin_(Transthyretin)- water soluble plasma protein. High in concentration and precipitated by full saturation with ammonium sulfate. Albumin serves function of transport of LCFA, bilirubin, bile acids, steroid hormones and many other metabolites, It also serves as amino acid pool. Its concentrations decrease in severe protein deficiency, liver diseases and nephritis. Globulins- soluble in saline and are separated by half- saturation with Ammonium sulfate. and can be categorized on basis of elctrophoretic separation into various fractions,-(α1- Antitrypsin, TBP, α2- Ceruloplasmin,β-Fibrinogen & gamma- Ab fraction). Globulins involved in transport of lipoproteins, vitamins etc. antibodies constitute gamma globulin fraction.

Half life of plasma proteins depends on glycosylated residue, receptor of which is present on surface of hepatocytes that pick old age plasma proteins and subjected to destruction.

**What is pH of blood?**

**Ans**- blood pH = 7.4 ± 0.2

**What is the function of RBC & why it known as red blood corpuscles?**

**Ans**- Red blood cells carry oxygen from the lungs to all cells of the body. Since mature RBC lack nucleus it is known as corpuscles. Average life span of RBC is of 120 days.

**What is Haemoglobin? Give structure and function of Hb.**

**Ans**- Hb is $O_2$ transport protein present in RBC and transport oxygen from lungs to different tissues. It is responsible for red color of blood. Hb consists of haeme & globin (protein portion 2-α & 2-β). Haeme consists of porphyrin (tetrapyrrole ring- four pyrrole rings joined by methane bridge) with central Iron ($Fe^{2+}$) atom in ferrous state. heme group attached to each chain, therefore $4O_2$ molecules binds to each Hb. Low blood level of Hb indicates anemic condition.

Normal Hb level for adult male 12-16 mg/dl and for female 11-15 mg/dl.

**What is hemoglobinopathies?**

**Ans**- Any abnormalities in structure of Hb (variant form of Hb), that is often inherited and may cause a blood disorder known as hemoglobinopathies.

- Sickle cell anemia- In this condition shape of RBC changes from normal biconcave to sickle. Sickle shape RBC blocks blood flow and consequently $O_2$ supply in narrow capillaries leading to pain (observed in joints) and destruction of RBC. This is due change of glutamic acid by valine at $6^{th}$ position of beta chain.
- Thalassemia-Inherited blood disorders where defects occurs in rate of synthesis of one or more Hb chains ( structure of chain remains normal) resulting into premature death of RBC and less count of healthy RBC in blood leading to anemia.
- β-thalassemia –In which synthesis of beta globin chain of Hb is defective or absent, in α-thalassemia defect is in synthesis of alpha chain.
- Thalassemia minor- (Trait) - out of two if one copy of gene is defective and one normal then this is known as minor. Minor have no anemia or mild anemia.
- Thalassemia major- Both copies of gene is defective then this leads severe anemic condition known as Thalassemia major and such patients needs regular blood transfusion.

**What is methaemoglobin?**

**Ans**- Condition which leads to change of normal ferrous ($Fe^{2+}$) to ferric state ($fe^{3+}$) state in one or more of the four iron atom in Hb is known as methaemoglobinemia and such Hb as methaemoglobin or ferrihaemoglobin. ferric state ($fe^{3+}$) Iron do not bind $O_2$ leads to anemia.

**What is carboxyhaemoglobin?**

**Ans**- Binding of and formation of stable complex between Hb and carbon monoxide is known as carboxyhaemoglobin (normaly present 1-2 %). CO have 200 times more affinity compared to $O_2$ for iron of Hb. Accidental inhalation (environmental pollutant/ smoking, etc) or endogenous production ( by product methylene chloride)produce CO and forms CO-Hb).

**What is sulfohaemoglobinemia?**

**Ans**- It's a rare condition in which there is excess sulfhemoglobin (SulfHb) in the blood. $H_2S$ combine with Iron of Haemoglobin.

**Which hormones play key role in regulating fluid and electrolyte balance?**

**Ans**- Antidiuretic hormone (ADH), aldosterone, Atrial natriuretic peptide (ANF).

**What is the function of white blood cells?**

**Ans**- WBC fights against infection and protect us from diseases.

**What is meant by hemoglobin?**

**Ans**- Iron containing ( $Fe^{2+}$) protein inside red blood cells that carries oxygen from lungs to tissue and organs in the body and carries $CO_2$ back to the lungs.

**What involves in the mechanism of coagulation?**

**Ans**-The mechanism of coagulation involves activation, adhesion, and aggregation of platelets as well as deposition and maturation of fibrin.

**What is blood coagulation?**

**Ans**- Damaged to vessel result into loss of blood, in order to minimize blood loss, thrombocytes aggregates to form loose clot (thrombus) for vessel contraction. This is known as haemostasis. This loose clot is soon deposited with polymeric meshwork of fibrin (formed from cleavage of souble fibrinogen by action of thrombin). This process of formation of clot (fibrin network) is known as coagulation or blood clotting and involves clotting factors and some High mol wt. lipoproteins.

**Clotting factors**

**Names**

I Fibrinogen

II Prothrombin

III Tissue factor/thromboplastin

IV $Ca^{2+}$
V Proaccelerin
VI -
VII Proconvertin
VIII Antihemophilic factor A
XI Christmas factor
X Stuart–Prower factor
XI Plasma thromboplastin antecedent
XII Hageman factor
XIII Fibrin-stabilizing factor

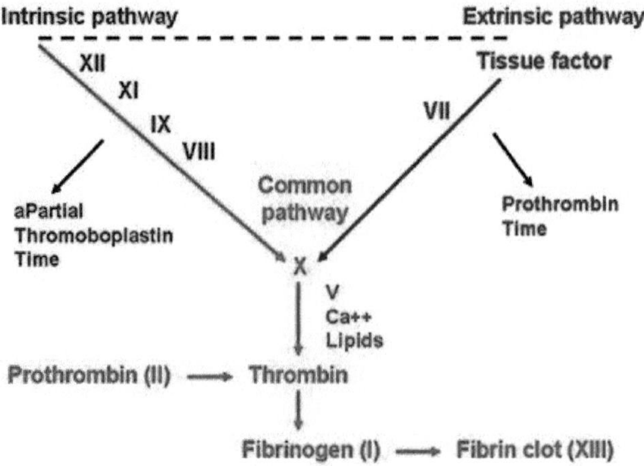


**Which component of the blood helps in blood coagulating?**

**Ans**- Platelets helps in the coagulation of the blood in a cut or wound by forming plug at site of bleeding and binds prothombin to convert it into thrombin and to form fibrin clot.

**How the clotting is regulated?**

**Ans**- It is regulated by synthesis of metabolites that doesn't allow clotting ex-antithrombin-III & Heparin (a natural anticoagulant) and prevents clot formation (by interfering with serine proteases) but does not dissolve clot. Whereas, Protein C ensures proteolytic degradation of factors V and VIII.

**What is fibrinolysis?**

**Ans**- Dissolution of blood clot (fibrin thrombus) is known as fibrinolysis. It is achieved through plasma serine protease known as Plasmin. Since plasmin is found in inactive form as Plasminogen it need to be activated and this activation is achieved by plasminogen activator. TPA - from vascular endothelia, urokinase from kidney. Heart attack treatment includes use of streptokinase a fibrinolytic enzyme from bacteria.

**Who devised ABO blood group system?**

**Ans**- Karl Landsteiner.

**What are blood group antigens?**

**Ans**- These are actually the oligosaccharides present on surface of blood cell and different for different individuals.

**How many blood groups are there in human being?**

**Ans**- There is four major blood groups namely A, B, AB, O. Antigens for blood groups A & B is tetrasaccharidess with difference of terminal residues as galactose or N-acetylgalactosamine respectively. AB blood groups have both (Ag- A and Ag-B). Blood group O arises from an oligosaccharide (the H antigen) that lacks the terminal residue of antigens A and B.

**Which antibodies are found in the plasma of a person with A blood group?**

**Ans**- Anti-B, but not anti A.

**What is Antiserum?**

**Ans**-Antiserum is a blood containing specific antibody.

**What is Acidosis and Alkalosis?**

**Ans**- Acidosis is a condition in which there is too much acid in the body fluid and Alkalosis is a condition in which there is too much base in the body fluids. pH of blood & body fluids is 7.4

maintain by buffering systems. This value, if reduced by 0.03 units this is known as acidosis and increase in this by 0.03 units known alkalosis.

**What is difference between metabolic / respiratory acidosis and alkalosis?**

**Ans**- Carbonate/bicarbonate buffering system is major in regulating pH of blood at 7.4 by regulating concentration of $pCO_2$ by lung and $HCO_3^-$ by kidney. If there is increase in $H^+$ concentration, due high pCO2 this is known as respiratory acidosis (breathing out less CO2) . Term respiratory indicates that $CO_2$ concentration mainly regulated by lungs). Low concentration of $H^+$ (increased pH value) due to lower pCO2 is known as respiratory alkalosis.

Similarly $HCO_3^-$ is regulated by kidney and therefore term metabolic is associated with their imbalance. Increased $HCO_3^-$ results in low $H^+$ (High pH value) such condition is known as metabolic alkalosis. And decreased $HCO_3^-$ results in high $H^+$ (Low pH value) such condition is known as metabolic acidosis (ex. serve diarrhea results in $HCO_3^-$ loss)

**What is hemophilia-A? What is Absence of which clotting factor leads to this condition?**

**Ans**- Absence of clotting factor-VIII (Antihaemophilic factor) leads to condition that does not allow clotting this condition is known as Haemophillia.

**Which blood cells secrets antibody?**

**Ans**- Antibody secreting cells are B-lymphocytes also known as Plasma cells.

**What is haemopoesis?**

**Ans**- It's a process of formation of blood corpuscles.

**How many liters of blood are there in average adult?**

**Ans**- Approximately 5-6 litres.

**What is acid-base hemostasis?**

**Ans**- Acid – base hemostasis is the hemostatic regulation of the pH of the body extracellular fluid.

**Name the clotting factor that is metal ion in nature.**

**Ans**- Factor IV (Calcium).

Clotting factors in blood is present in inactive precursor form called zymogen. These precursors need activation and once activated, activate another Inactive form into active form and so on. Blood clotting occurs in series of enzymatic reaction and follows cascade mechanism (1 A activates 10 B, each B activates 10 C so producing 100 C from single A) to produce magnification at each step to achieve clotting in effective time followed by injury. Seven of the clotting factors are serine proteases and calcium is the only factor that is metal.

**What is Intrinsic & extrinsic pathway of coagulation?**

**Ans**- Two routes exist for blood clot formation. The

Extrinsic pathway is initiated by factor-III (tissue thromboplastin factor) released from injured tissues, which activates coagulation factor VII. Active VIIa generates the active factors IXa and Xa from their precursors. With the aid of factor VIIIa, Phospholipid, and $Ca^{2+}$, factor IXa produces additional Xa, which finally— with the support of Va, PL, and Ca2+—releases active thrombin.

Intrinsic pathway is instigated when the blood comes into physical contact with abnormal surfaces caused by injury. Pathway takes place in five steps via factors XIIa, XIa, IXa, and Xa to the activation of prothrombin. Both pathways merge at Factor X and culminate in clot formation.

# VIII

# Hormones

**What do you mean by hormone?**

**Ans**: A chemical substance produced by certain organs transported through body fluids such as blood or sap and binds to specific receptors on target tissue to stimulate specific action.

**What type of hormone Hypothalamic are?**

**Ans:** Hypothalamic hormones are peptides; they are secreted by the hypothalamus.

**Why the receptor for estrogen is intracellular?**

**Ans**: Estrogen, a hormone secreted by the ovaries. Since, it is a steroid in nature, can easily pass through the lipid bilayer of the cell membrane. Thus its receptor is intracellular.

**A gland which secretes both hormone and enzyme is.**

**Ans:** Pancreas is the gland that secretes both hormone and enzyme.

**Which gland produces Insulin & what is function of it?**

**Ans:** β- cells of pancreas secrete insulin that helps to lower blood glucose level.

**What is the exact location of pituitary gland?**

**Ans**: Pituitary gland is located at the base of midbrain below hypothalamus.

**Why Pituitary gland called as the master gland?**

**Ans:** Because it secretes hormones that regulate activities of other endocrine glands.

**Explain the term tropic hormone?**

**Ans:** Tropic hormones are the group of hormones which influence other endocrine glands to produce hormones.

**What is the main hormone secreted by the Thyroid gland?**

**Ans**: Thyroid gland lies in front of Larynx. Triiodothyronine (T3) and thyroxine (T4) are the hormones secreted by the Thyroid gland. Deficiency of $T_3$ produces cretinism in children & myxoedema in adults.

**Name the amino acid which is the precursor for the synthesis of thyroid hormones?**

**Ans:** Tyrosine is the amino acid which is the precursor for the synthesis of thyroid hormones.

**What is the name of disorder caused by excess production of thyroid hormone?**

**Ans:** Exophthalmic goitre is a disorder which is caused by excess production of thyroid hormone.

**What is PTH?**

**Ans**- Its parathyroid hormone secreted by Parathyroid gland (back of thyroid) regulate Calcium phosphorus balance in blood. Deficiency cause cramps excess weakens bone.

**Name the hormone known as flight and fight hormone?**

**Ans:** Adrenaline (epinephrine) is known as flight and fight hormone. During stressful conditions adrenaline is released into the blood sending impulses to organs to create a specific response.

**What is the name of the cells producing the hormone in adrenal medulla?**

**Ans**: Chromaffin cells are present in the adrenal medulla; they are innervated by the splanchnic nerve and secret adrenaline.

**Low level of adrenal cortex hormones result into?**

**Ans**: Low level of adrenal cortex hormones result in Addison disease. It is fewer than 1 million cases per year in India.

**What is source of Gonadotropic hormone?**

**Ans**: Adenohypophysis is also known as anterior pituitary. Adenohypophysis secretes gonadotropic hormone and it is released in gonads.

**Which of the following hormone is responsible for the secretion of milk after parturition?**

**Ans:** Prolactin is responsible for the secretion of milk after parturition. It is also known as the luteotropic hormone.

**Corpus luteum develops from.**

**Ans**: Corpus luteum develops from an ovarian follicle during the luteal phase of menstrual cycle. Corpus luteum secretes Progesterone and estrogen.

**What is the function of LH hormone?**

**Ans**: LH hormone is luteinizing hormone. It is produced in pituitary gland. It stimulates the production of testosterone in males.

**What is a male sex hormone?**

**Ans:** Androgen is a male sex hormone. It primarily influences the growth and development of the male reproductive system.

**What is not a major endocrine organ, but produces hormones in addition to its major function?**

**Ans:** Kidney cells produce the hormones renin and erythropoietin, but their primary function is excretion of body waste.

**What is cortisol and its function?**

**Ans**: Cortisol is a steroid hormone, it is called a stress hormone and its function is to helps in metabolism and immune response.

**What are steroidal hormones?**

**Ans-** These liphophilic compounds regulate cellular reactions (growth, development, metabolism).

progesterone, cortisol, aldosterone, testosterone, estradiol, and calcitriol.

# IX

# Chromatography

**Define chromatography.**

**Ans**-Chromatography is a separation technique in which the complex mixture are separated into two phases: a stationary phase with a large surface area, and a mobile phase. The goal of the stationary phase is to delay the passage of the sample components. When components pass through the system at different speeds, they separate at certain times. Each component has a characteristic time to pass through the system, called the retention time. Chromatographic separation is achieved when the retention time of the analyte differs from the rest of the components of the sample. Chromatography is one of the main analytical methods and allows the separation and quantification of substances that are very similar in structure and its chemical properties.

**Define Analyte.**

**Ans**- It is a product of a chromatographic process.

**What is Analytical Chromatography?**

**Ans**- It is used to determine the presence and concentration of analyte in the sample.

**What is Preparative Chromatography?**

**Ans**- It is used for the purification of substances for specific purposes (for analysis).

**Define Chromatogram.**

**Ans-** It is a visual representation or results of the chromatographic process. Each substance corresponds to a certain peak on the chromatogram.

**Define Chromatograph.**

**Ans-** Instrument for carrying out chromatography.

**What is holding time?**

**Ans-** Time during which the analyte passes through the chromatographic system under certain conditions.

**Define Stationary phase.**

**Ans-** Substance that is attached to the column or to the panel, on whose surface the substances are separated.

**Define Mobile phase.**

**Ans-** Phase that is moving in a certain direction. It can be a liquid or gas. The mobile phase moves through a column that carries the sample to be separated.

**Chromatography is a physical method that is used to separate what?**

**Ans-** Complex mixtures.

**Ion exchange chromatography is based on which type of attraction?**

**Ans-** Electrostatic attraction.

**Chromatography with solid stationary phase is called which chromatography?**

**Ans-** Adsorption chromatography.

**Define Chromatogram.**

**Ans-** The pattern on the paper in chromatography is called chromatogram.

**Which HPLC detectors is used as a bulk property or general purpose detector?**

**Ans-** Evaporative Light scattering detector.

**Thin layer chromatography is which chromatography?**

**Ans-** Adsorption chromatography.

**In which type of chromatography, the stationary phase is held in a narrow tube and the mobile phase is forced through it under pressure?**

**Ans-** Column chromatography.

**What is Eluent ?**

**Ans-** It is a solvent that used for separation of absorbed material from stationary phase.

**In chromatography, mobile phase can be made of?**

**Ans-** Liquid or gas.

**In size exclusion chromatography, solute molecules are separated on the bases of?**

**Ans-** Molecular geometry and size.

**HPLC is an abbreviation for?**

**Ans-** High Pressure Liquid Chromatography.

**The process of passing a mobile phase through a chromatography column is called which one of the following?**

**Ans-** Elution.

# X

# Spectrophotometry

**What is Spectrophotometry?**

**Ans-** It is concerned with the quantitative measurement of the absorption or transmission properties of a material as a function of light wavelength.

**What is Lambert-Beer Law ?**

**Ans-** When a beam of monochromatic light is allowed to pass through a solution, its absorption is directly proportional to concentration of the solution (number of solutes in a solvent) & It's path length (distance to which light traveled in solution), commonly a diameter of cuvette).

Absorbance A = $-\log I/ I_0$ = ecd

e-absorption coefficient

c- concentration

d- path lenth

**What factors causes a deviation from beers law?**

**Ans-** Concentrated solution, molecular aggregation, polychromatic light, stray radiations, etc.

**What is the difference between colorimeter & spectrophotometre**?

**Ans-** A colorimeter has range of visible region (400-750nm) and spectrophotometre posses working range in uv- visible region (200-750 nm).

**Give the components & functions of colorimeter/ spectrophotometer.**

**Ans-** The parts of a colorimeter are:

Radiation source - Tungsten filament lamp used in visible region and deuterium/ lamp or mercury vapour lamp used for UV region. Nerns't glover & gober used in Infra Red specctoscopy.

Monochromators - a device that resolved polychromatic light into monochromatic (consists of single wavelength) light. It consists of entrance slit for radiation entry followed by Prism or difractional gratings or both and exit slit for coming out of monochromatic light.

Sample holder (cuvette)- Material intended to hold sample generally made of glass in colorimeter but replaced with quartz in case of spectrometre.

Detectors- photocells, phototubes, etc. used to measure the amount of light transmitted (coming out of solution) and or absorbed light.

Display unit meter to display the output from the detector.

**What is the unit of absorbance which can be derived from Beer Lambert's law?**

**Ans-** Absorbance has no unit. The units of absorptivity, distance, and concentration cancel each other. Hence, absorption has no unit.

**Why sample holder (cuvette) used in spectrometer is made of quartz rather than glass?**

**Ans-** Glass absorbs UV lights and gives false absorption hence, glass replace with quartz.

**What is not required in single beam absorption instruments?**

**What is double beam spectrometer?**

**Ans-** Beam splitter/chopper splits beam into two equal intensity beams. One passes through the sample and other through the reference. Double beam spectrometers avoid errors due to fluctuation.

**What is dual wavelength spectrometer? Give advantage of it.**

**Ans-** It uses two different wavelengths. This allows continuous monitoring of reaction if substrate & products have different $\lambda$ max.

**What is use of Mass spectrometers?**

**Ans**- Mass spectrometer is used to determine the relative mass of atoms and molecules. In mass spectrometer, the sample which is to be analyzed is bombarded with electrons. As a result, ions are produced.

**Define molar absorptivity and give its unit.**

**Ans**- A measure of how strongly a chemical species absorbs light at a particular wavelength. It is often expressed in units of $cm^{-1}M^{-1}$.

**What is transmittance?**

**Ans**- The fraction of incident light that gets transmitted through a medium is called as transmittance (T) of that medium.

**What is optical density/OD?**

**Ans**- The logarithmic ratio of the intensity of incident light (Io) to that of the transmitted light I is called as optical density.

**Define absorptivity?**

**Ans**- Absorbance of a solution having concentration of 1gm/dm3 (equivalent to 1 Mol) placed in a Cell of 1 cm thickness is called absorptivity.

**Define λ max?**

**Ans**- The wavelength at which a solution shows maximum absorbance is called as λ max.

**Why spectrometry uses λ max for quantitative measurements?**

**Ans**- Variation in concentration of material shows maximum change at λ max among the range it absorbed.( absorption spectrum).

**Give two applications of spectrophotometer?**

**Ans**- Detection of concentration of substances, Characterization of proteins, check of adulteration, purity etc.

# XI

# pH and buffer

**Who gave the concept of pH?**

**Ans-** Sorensen.

**What is the pH ?**

**Ans-** Scale used to specify the acidity or basicity of a solution. pH denoting 'potential of hydrogen' or 'power of hydrogen')

$pH = -\log [H^+]$.

**What is biological Importance of pH?**

**Ans-** The pH can control the availability, absorption of nutrients, biological functions, microbial activity, and the behavior of chemicals.

**Why the pH scale is from 0 to 14?**

**Ans-** One far end is not more than 1M of hydrogen ions, which results in a pH value of not more than 0. While on the other end is not more than 1M of hydroxide ions which results in a pH value of not more than 14.

**What is the pH range for acids?**

**Ans-** pH scale ranges from 0 to 14, with 7 being neutral. pH less than 7 are acidic, while pH greater than 7 are alkaline.

**What is pH of pure water?**

**Ans-** pH of pure water is 7. In pure water, the concentration of $H^+$ and $OH^-$ ions are equal to $10^{-7}$.

**What is pKa value?**

**Ans-** The pKa value is used to indicate the strength of an acid. pKa is the negative log of the acid dissociation constant or Ka value.

**What is pka value for strong acid?**

**Ans-** A lower pKa value indicates a stronger acid. That is, the lower value indicates the acid more fully dissociates in water.

**What is buffer?**

**Ans-** A buffer is solution which resists change in pH. It consist of a weak acid and its conjugate base or a weak base and its conjugate acid. Acetate buffer contains acetic acid ($CH_3COOH$) & sodium acetate ($CH_3COONa$).

**What are different type of biological buffers / buffer systems?**

**Ans-** The three major buffer systems of our body are carbonate/ bicarbonate, phosphate, plasma protein & Hb buffer system.

carbonate/bicarbonate- Important buffer contributing 75 % total blood buffering. It consists of $CO_2$, $H_20$, $H_2CO_3$ & $HCO3^-$ and enzyme cabonic anhydrase catalyzing reaction

$CO_2 + H_2O$ ------ $H_2\ CO_3$-------- $H+ + HCO_3^-$.

At pH value of blood plasma $HCO_3^-$ and $CO_2$ are present in a ratio of about 20 : 1. $CO_2$ in solution also in equilibrium with gaseous $CO_2$ in lung. $CO_2/HCO_3$ ratio and consequently blood pH can be altered by increase or decreasing $CO_2$ release in lungs by slow & fast respiration.

Phosphate- ($H_2PO_4/HPO_42^-$) also contributes to the buffering capacity of the blood plasma Although, to a lesser extent (1%) due to low concentration of phosphate in blood.

Protein & Hb- The buffering effect of plasma proteins involves contributions from all of the ionizable side chains of constituting amino acid residues, especially acidic ( Asp & Glut) and Basic (histidine). Contribute about 24 % of total blood buffering.

**What are the factors that affect buffer capacity?**

**Ans-** First isratio of salt to acid ([$A^-$]/[HA). The buffer capacity is optimal when the ratio is 1:1; that is, when pH = pKa. Second factor is total buffer concentration. For example, it will take more acid or base to deplete a 0.5 M buffer than a 0.05 M buffer.

**Give Henderson Hasselbalch equation?**

**Ans**- The buffer pH can be estimated using the Henderson-Hasselbalch equation, which is

pH = pKa + log ([A-]/[HA])

**Do weak acid ionize at high pH?**

**Ans**- An acid or base's strength refers to its degree of ionization. A strong acid (HCl) will completely ionize in water while a weak acid ($CH_3COOH$) will only partially ionize.

# XII

# Bioenergetics

**What is sequence of aerobic respiration?**

**Ans-** Glycolysis, Tricarboxylic acid cycle & Electron Transport Chain.

**Give the equation for aerobic respiration.**

**Ans-** $C_6H_{12}O_6$ $6O_2 + 6H_2 0 = 6CO_2 + 12$ $H_2O$+686 Kcal.

**What is Glycolysis?**

**Ans-** Process of enzyme mediated conversion of single molecules of glucose (6-Carbon) into two molecules of pyruvate (3-carbon). It also called EMP (Embeden, Mayerhoff, Paranas pathway).

**What is the location of glycolysis in a eukaryotic cell?**

**Ans-** Cytosol.

**Which of the following enzyme catalyzes the first step of glycolysis?**

**Ans-** Hexokinase (acts on hexoses & requires $Mg^{2+}$ ion).

**What is the first step in the payoff phase of glycolysis?**

**Ans-** Glycolysis initially required energy in the form of 2 ATP to prepare glucose for further energy extraction this is known aspreparatory phase/ investment phase. Later phase is known as pay off phase that begins with oxidation of glyceraldehyde 3-phosphate to 1, 3-bisphosphoglycerate.

**What is net gain of ATP in glycolysis?**

**Ans-** In glycolysis, net gain of ATP is 8 (total 10 ATP are produced but 2ATP utilized in preparatory phase in first & third reaction of phosphorylation).

**How much ATPs are produced from 1 gm mole of glucose if subjected to aerobic respiration?**

**Ans-** 38 ATP.

**Which is committed step for sugar to undergo glycolysis?**

**Ans-** Third reaction of glycolysis which converts fructose-6-phosphate to fructose-1,6-bisphosphate ( bis-indicate two phosphate groups are separated) & catalyzed by phosphofructokinaseis committed to glycolysis. Initial two products Glu-6-phosphate and fruct-6-phosphate can play roles in other pathways, but fructose-1,6-bisphosphate does not. After fructose-1,6-bisphosphate is formed from the original sugar, no other pathways are available, and the molecule must undergo glycolysis.

**Which are the control points in glycolysis?**

**Ans-** Glycolysis is regulated or control at three steps. First catalysed by hexokinase glucose to glucose-6-phosphate, second, catalysed by phosphofructokinase fructose -6-phosphate to fructose-1,6-*bis*phosphate and the last is the reaction of PEP to pyruvate, catalyzed by pyruvate kinase .

**What are the possible fates of pyruvate after glycolysis?**

**Ans-** Pyruvate under aerobic condition oxidize to $CO_2$ & $H_20$ (through TCA & ETC). In anaerobic condition undergoes fermentation. Alcoholic fermentation Pyruvate loses carbon dioxide to produce acetaldehyde by pyruvate decarboxylase (requires $Mg^{2+}$ & TPP- thiamine pyrophosphate coenzyme). Acetaldehyde in turn, is reduced to produce ethanol by Alcohol dehydrogenase. Lactic acid fermentation occurs if pyruvate produces lactate. Ex- contracting muscles.

$$\underset{\text{Pyruvate}}{CH_3-C(=O)-C(=O)-O^-} + NADH + H^+ \underset{\text{Lactate dehydrogenase}}{\rightleftharpoons} \underset{\text{Lactate}}{CH_3-CH(OH)-C(=O)-O^-} + NAD^+$$

**Fates of pyruvate**

**What is difference between substrate level phosphorylation & oxidative phosphorylation?**

**Ans-** Catalysis of molecules (Ex-glucose) results into production of energy in the form of ATP, which is formed by addition of phosphate group (phosphorylation) to ADP. If ATP produce directly at the level of substrate is known as substrate level phosphorylation. Energy produces indirectly as reducing equivalents (NADH/FADH), which, after passing through ETC gives ATP- known as oxidative phosphorylation.

**Why aerobic respiration more advantageous than anaerobic?**

**Ans-** Reducing equivalents (NADH) produced in glycolysis is utilized to produce different metabolites under anaerobic conditions and hence cannot available to produce energy. Therefore anaerobic respiration produces less energy compared to aerobic.

**Whenever the cell's ATP supply is depleted, which of the following enzyme's activity is increased?**

**Ans-** Phosphofructokinase-1.

**Explain the regulation of glycolysis?**

**Ans-** Primarily hormone Insulin activates glycolysis whereas glucagon inhibit it. Epinephrine shows different effect in muscle turn on and turn off in liver. High glucose and high energy signal inhibit glycolysis and Low glucose and low energy signal activates.

**What are different Inhibitors of glycolysis?**

**Ans-** Idoacetate- Blocks there action catalyzed by glyceraldehydes-3-phosphate dehydrogenase.

Fluoride - blocks the reaction catalyzed by Enolase.

Arsenate - is phosphate analogues and bind with Glyceraldehyde-3-P dehydrogenase forming arsenate derivative of 1,3,diphosphoglycerate which is quite unstable and form 3 phosphoglycerate. This continues with glycolysis but results in loss of ATP.

**What is galactosemia?**

**Ans-** Galactosemia is rare hereditary disorder that results in impaired metabolism of galactose (unable to processe it) due to deficiency of enzymes galactokinase or galactose-1-Phoshpate-uridyl transferase, results in to accumulation of galactose. Symptoms includes vomiting, weight loss, yellow skin and white eyes etc. if left untreated can be life threatening. Gal converted to alcohol galactitolthat accumulates in soft tissues of eyes causing cataract.

**Why Krebs cycle is known as TCA or citric acid cycle & what is its location in a cell?**

**Ans-** Kreb's cycle named after its discoverer Hans Kreb. Since, the first product of cycle is citrate it also known as citric acid cycle. Citrate possesses three carboxylic (COOH) group therefore also name as tricarboxylic acid cycle TCA. It is occur in mitochondria.

**What is role of TCA in metabolism?**

**Ans-** TCA comprises combination of a molecule of acetyl Co-A with Oxaloacetate(OAA) resulting in formation of 6-C tricarboxylic acid (citrate). This involves series of reactions that leads to release of lot of energy (1 GTP= 1ATP, 3 NADH= 09 ATP, 1 FADH=2ATP

Total= 12 from acetyl CoA & 15 from pyruvate ) 2 mol of $CO_2$ with regeneration of OAA.

**Why TCA is known as convergent /common pathway of oxidation?**

**Ans**- It is final common pathway for oxidation of carbohydrates, lipids and proteins. This is because glucose, fatty acids and amino acids are all metabolized to acetyl Co-A or intermediates of TCA.

**Why TCA is amphibolic?**

**Ans**- TCA or the Krebs cycle is amphibolic as it serves not only as catabolic/degrading pathway but also anabolic pathway (formation of new compounds from intermediates of cycle ex. Gluconeogenesis, amino acid synthesis etc).

**What is anaplerotic reaction? Is TCA anaplerotic?**

**Ans**- Anaplerotic reactions are chemical reactions that form intermediates of a metabolic pathway.TCA is anaplerotic in nature as it replenish (fill up) its intermediates. Enzymes pyruvate carboxylase replenishes the TCA cycle intermediates in animals by converting pyruvate to OAA whenever TCA is diminished of intermediates.

**Which coenzymes take part in TCA and from which vitamin it is produced?**

**Ans**- Riboflavin –FAD- alpha ketoglutarate dH complex,

Niacin – NAD- Isocitrate dH, alpha ketoglutarate dH, malate dH. Thiamine-TDP- involves in decarboxylation in α-ketoglutarate dehydrogenase reaction.

Pantothenic acid as part of Co-A.

**Is the activity of aconitase (2$^{nd}$ enzyme of cycle) is sterospecific?**

**Ans**- Citrate though not posses chiral carbon but isocitarte has 2 and therefore have four different form but due to sterospecificity of aconitase only one form produced only.

**Which reaction of TCA produced direct GTP/ATP equivalent?**

**Ans**- Reaction catalyzed by action of succinyl Co-A synthetase produced GTP, which can be converted into ATP by a nucleoside diphosphate kinase.

**What is ETC?**

**Ans**- Electron transport chain is series of electron carriers located in inner mitochondrial membrane.

**What is cristae?**

**Ans**- Mitochondria is double membrane organelle. It Its inner membrane undergoes infoldings known as cristae.

**What is the sequence of electron acceptor in ETC?**

Ans:

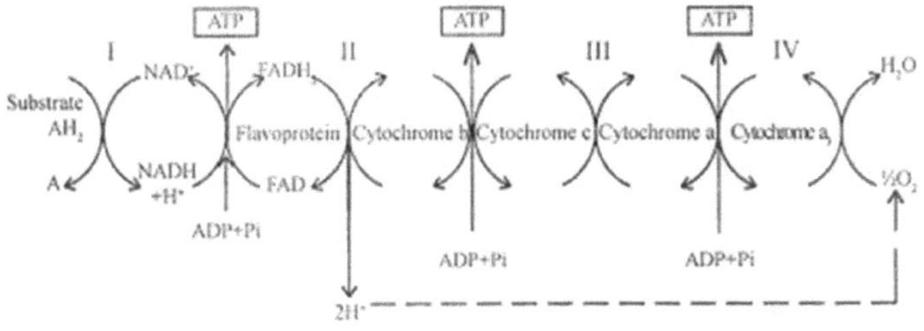

Electron Transport Chain

**What is function of ETC?**

**Ans**- ETC generated energy (ATP) by oxidative phosphorylation and regenerate reducing equivalents. Reducing equivalents (NADH/ FADH via QH2) get oxidized by transferring their electrons to carriers/components of ETC which itself becomes oxidized by transferring electrons to next carrier and finaly to oxygen to form water.

**What is chemiosmotic hypothesis?**

**Ans**- Energy released during transfer of electrons through electron carrier used to transport protons out from matrix to intermembrane space creating proton gradient in matrix. Only way for proton to come back to matrix is through $F_OF_1$/ ATP synthetase complex that uses this proton motive force for phosphorylation of ADP to ATP. This synthesis of ATP due to chemiosmotic gradient of proton is known as chemiosmotic hypothesis given by peter Mitchell.

**What are the different complexes of ETC/respiratory chain?**

**Ans-** Respiratory chain consists protein complexes,

Complex-I is NADH dehydrogenase,

Complex –III is cytochrome c reductase, and complex IV is cytochrome oxidase. Succinate dehydrogenase (SDH) is said to be complex-II (an enzyme of TCA) and $F_0F_1$/ ATP synthase is complex-V.

**Which are the mobile carrier molecules of respiratory chain?**

**Ans-** Ubiquinone (coenzyme Q- its non protein component) and cytochrome.

**How many protons is transport out from matrix to intermembrane space?**

**Ans-** 10 protons are moved out from matrix $4H^+$ each at complex –I & III and $2H^+$ at complex-IV For one molecule of water formed.

**Describe ATP synthase/ $F_0F_1$ ATPase.**

**Ans-** $F_0F_1$ ATPase is consists of two parts. $F_0$ is named so, due to its sensitivity to Oligomycin. $F_0$ portion is consists of 12 transmembrane c and 1 a-subunits. It is present in the membrane and forms a channel for the movement of proton. Another part is head like catalytic unit F1 which emerges out from membrane into matrix, consists of 3 $\alpha$ and 3 $\beta$ subunits arranged alternately. Single gamma and epsilon subunit present between $F_0$& $F_1$. Beta and delta peptides also present.

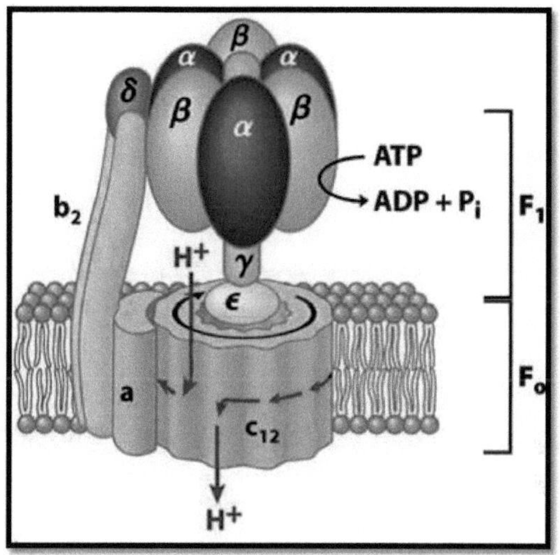


**ATP synthase**

**How $F_0F_1$ ATPase synthesize ATP?**

**Ans-** ATPase contains three sites with ADP and Pi bound at first, at second site consists of bonds formed and at third formed ATP is released. Downward movements of proton provide the energy used to form ATP from ADP & Pi.

**What is P:O ratio?**

**Ans-** Number of ATP equivalents formed per 2 electrons moving through ETC is known as P:O ratio.

**What is ATP translocase & what is its function?**

**Ans-** ATP translocase is protein present in mitochondrial membrane. It involved in exchange of mitochondrial ATP to cytosol for inward of cytosolic ADP to mitochondria. This ensures continues production of ATP and make ATP available at site distant from its production.

**What is uncoupler of ETC/ respiratory chain?**

**Ans**- Uncouplers are substances which do not allow oxidation to couple with phosphorylation of ADP. In this case electron transport continues with oxygen consumption but without production of ATP (phosphorylation of ADP). Uncouplers work by dissipating pH gradient. Ex, 2, 4 Dinitrophenol is lipohilic in nature and cross inner mitochondrial membrane releasing proton in matrix thus, destroying proton gradient and no ATP formation. Valinomycin is another example of uncoupler. Thermogenin present in brown fat tissues of newborn also work similarly and produce heat without ATP production.

**What is inhibitor for ETC?**

**Ans**- Inhibitors are substances that block flow of electorns and ATP production. Different inhibitors have different blocking site in the chain. Electron carriers before block are reduced and after block are oxidized. Ex- Rotenone- block at NADH dehydogenase keeping NADH reduced but FAD continues producing 2 ATPs. Cyanide blocks transfer of electrons to $O_2$. Attractyloside block ADP/ATP translocase. Oligomycinblock ADP phosphorylation. Antimycin bllock cytochorme b to cyt C1.

## Inhibitors of Oxidative Phosphorylation

- Complex I: Rotenone
- Complex II: Carboxin
- Complex III: Antimycin A
- Complex IV: Cyanide, Azide, Carbon monoxide
- ATP synthase: Oligomycin
- ATP-ADP translocase: Atractyloside (a plant glycoside)

**What is hexose monophosphate shunt?**

**Ans-** Its pentose phosphate pathway or HMP shunt or alternatively phosphogluconate pathway. This is an alternative pathway for glucose metabolism begins with Glu-6-P.

**What is the significance of of HMP?**

**Ans-** HMP shunt produces Pentoses- required in synthesis of nucleic acids and NADPH that is required for fatty acid biosynthesis.

**What is gluconeogenesis?**

**Ans-** The process of synthesis of glucose or glycogen from non-carbohydrate precursor is known as gluconeogenesis.

**What is site for gluconeogenesis?**

**Ans-** Primarily organs involved are liver & kidney. Reactions for gluconeogenesis mainly takes in cytosol although, mitochondria also partly involved.

**What are the different substrates used for gluconeogenesis?**

**Ans-** Pyruvate, glycerol, lactate, glycogenic amino acids & TCA cycle intermediates are substrates for this process.

**How many ATP required for synthesis of glucose from 2 molecules of pyruvate or lactate.**

**Ans-** 6 ATP are needed.

**Gluconeogenesis is reverse of glycolysis?**

**Ans-** Though gluconeogenesis utilized seven of the ten glycolytic enzymes. It is not the reverse of glycolysis as it provides alternative path for 3 different enzymes of glycolysis.

**What are 3 bypass reactions of gluconeogenesis?**

**Ans-** a. First Bypass from pyruvate to PEP (pyruvate kinase) – pyruvate carboxylase convert pyruavte to oxaloacetate (OAA) this reaction requires $CO_2$ and consume ATP. OAA converted to malate and moves out of mitochondria regenerates OAA in cytosol that is converted to PEP by PEP carboxykinase using GTP hydrolysis to GDP.

b. Second bypass (phosphofructokinase)- dephosphorylation of fructose 1,6 bisphosphate to fructose-6-phosphate by fructose 1,6 bisphosphatase.

c.Third bypass (hexokinase)- reaction catalysed by Glucose-6-phosphatase converts Glu-6-P to Glucose.

**What is futile cycle?**

**Ans-** Futile means waste. If two reactions (one synthetic & one degradative) occurs simultaneously at a high rate in same cell leads to wastage of large amount of energy (ATP). Such ATP degrading cycle is termed as futile cycle. In some species futile cycle occurs for heat production.

**Give example of futile cycle.**

**Ans-**

hexokinase catalyses

ATP + Glucose à Glucose-6-P + ADP

Bypass counterpart in gluconeogenesis

glucose-6-phosphates cat.

Glucose-6-P + $H_2 0$ à Glucose + Pi

Sum of both reactions is

ATP à ADP + Pi

**What is glycogenesis and what is its function?**

**Ans-** The process of synthesis of glycogen from glucose is known glyocogenesis. This process ensures storage of glucose and its release on demand.

**What is site for glycogenesis?**

**Ans-** In cytosol of liver it supply glucose to blood and in skeletal muscle for energy requiring processes.

**Why muscle glycogen do not contribute to blood glucose?**

**Ans-** Muscles lacks Glu-6-phosphatase hence do not contribute.

**Which enzyme is involved in glycogenesis?**

**Ans-** Glycogen synthase is involved in glycogenesis. This enzyme adds glucosyl residue from UDP-Glu to non-reducing end of glycogen branches.( c-4 end of previously bound glycogen) Alpha 1,4 à1,6 transglycosylase initiate new branch.

**What is primer for glycogenesis?**

**Ans-** Protein glycogenin acts as primer and initiates glycogen synthesis, to which first incoming glucose molecule bind.

**What is cost of glycogenesis?**

**Ans**- TwoATPs are required to store each molecule of glucose into glycogen.

**What is glycogenolysis?**

**Ans**- Breakdown of glycogen is known as glycogenolysis. Whenever cell is deficient of glucose it is supplied by breakdown of glycogen. No ATP is required to remove glucose from glycogen.

**Name the enzyme involved in glycogenolysis.**

**Ans**- Glycogen phosphorylase that removes glucose as Glu-6-P form non-reducing end of unbranched (linear) glycogen chain.

**Why there is need for debranching enzyme in glycogenolyis?**

**Ans**- Glycogen phosphorylase unable to break glycogen when it reaches 4 residues apart from branching point then debranching enzymes come into action removes 3 glucose unit and add to next chain, and one glucose at branching point removed as free.

**Which enzyme catalysis the only reversible reaction of whole glycogen metabolism?**

**Ans**- Phosphoglucomutase.

**What is cori cycle?**

**Ans**- In muscle, If glycolysis occur at faster rate produce high amount of pyruvate which cannot metabolize aerobically through TCA and converted to lactate. Lactate transported to liver via blood where it is converted back to glucose by gluconeogenesis and pass to muscule. This interconversion of glucose to lactate in muscule and lactate to glucose by liver is known as cori cycle.

# XIII

# Mechanism of enzyme action

**What is the site for fatty acid synthesis?**

**Ans**- In human fatty acids are synthesized in Liver and adipose cytoplasm.

**Which enzymes are involve in fatty acids biosynthesis ?**

**Ans**- Fatty acid biosynthesis involves two cytoplasmic enzymes namely Acety Co-A carboxylase and fatty acid synthase complex.

**Describe the fatty acid synthase complex & significance of multifunctional systems ?**

**Ans**- Fatty Acid synthase complex is dimer of identical 250 kd multifunctional polypeptides arranged in head to tail fashion. Each of the subunits is a multienzyme complex of seven enzymes and the acyl carrier protein component. This multifunctional system has advantage in the sense that side reaction are prevented, low diffusion intermediates, and product of first is substrate for second increase efficiency.

**What is requirement of fatty acid synthesis?**

**Ans**- FA synthesis beside acetyl Co-A requires NADPH, ATP, $Mn^{2+}$, Biotin, pantothenic acid & $HCO^3$.

**How fatty acids biosynthesis take place?**

**Ans-** Fatty acid are synthesized as plamitate (C-16). This requires 1 acetyl Co-A and 7 malonyl CoA in addition to cofactors and coenzymes .

1. Acetyl Co-A carboxylase converts acetyl Co-A to malonyl Co-A. This reaction uses biotin as coenzyme, ATP and Bicarbonate ion ($CO_2$).

$HCO3^-$ + biotin-enzyme + ATP → CO2-biotin-enzyme + ADP + Pi

$CO_2$-biotin-enzyme +acetyl CoA→Malonyl CoA +biotin-enzyme

2. Fatty acid synthase complex catalayzes assembly of pyruvate from 1acetyl & 7 malony Co-A.

a. The acetyl group from acetyl Co-A binds with Cys-SH group of the β-ketoacyl-ACP synthase catalyzes by acetyl-CoA–ACP transacetylase.

b. In other reaction catalyzed by malonyl-CoA–ACP transferase, malonyl group from malonyl co-A binds with acyl carrier protein (ACP-SH)

3. Condensation – acetyl group combines with malonyl –ACP to form acetoacetyl ACP. This reaction results in release of $CO_2$ from malonyl group.(C- introduced by $HCO_3^-$) forming 4-carbon acetoacetyl group attached with ACP-SH. Enzyme β-Ketoacyl ACP synthase catalyze the reaction.

4. Next is reduction of of acetoacetyl-ACP at carbon -3 to form hydroxybutyryl-ACP by β-ketoacyl -ACP reductase . NADPH is use in this reaction.

5. Dehydaration- removal of water by hydroxybutyryl-ACP dehydratase from C-2 & C-3 to form trans-2- butenoyl-ACP.

6. Reduction by Enoyl –ACP reductase form butyryl-ACP .NADPH is electron donor.

This four carbon fragment attached with SH group of ACP transferred to Cys-SH, so that vacant ACP-SH group now take up another incoming malonyl Co-A and and the cycle is repeated (condensation, reduction, dehydaration and further reduction) until the acyl chain grows to C16. When the growing fatty acid reaches a chain length of 16 carbons, the acyl group is hydrolyzed to give the free fatty acid.

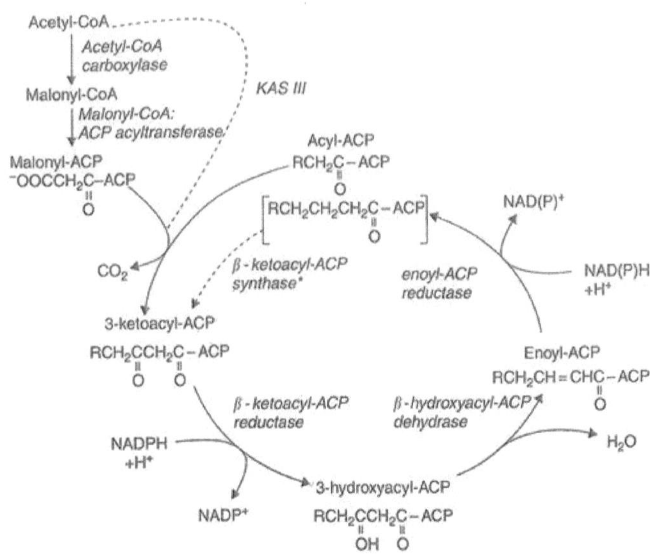


**How fatty acid synthesis is regulated?**

**Ans-** Acetyl Co-A carboxylase is key enzyme in regulation of fatty acid synthesis. Primary signal is insulin which activates acetyl Co-A carboxylase by dephosphorylation (short term) and induction of synthesis. In long term Glucagon, epinephrine (adrenaline) and phosphorylation have opposite effect and turn off biosynthesis of fatty acids.

Secondary signal includes Citrate which activates enzymes and long chian fatty acyl Co-A inhibits it.

**What is cost for synthesis of fatty acid (palmitate)?**

**Ans-** Fatty acid synthesis need acetyl CoA which must be transported from Mitochondria to cytosl. ( acetyl Co-A converted to citrate and comes out of mitochondria to cytosol, where it again converted back to Acetyl Co-A).

**Give the equation for synthesis of fatty acid palmitate?**

**Ans**- Acetyl-CoA + 7 Malonyl-CoA + 14NADPH +14H$^+$ à
C16 fatty acid +14NADP$^+$+ 7CO2 + 8CoA

**If palmitate is the product of fatty acid synthesis then how other long chain fatty acid are formed?**

**Ans**- Palmitate, the product of fatty acid synthase is further subjected to elongation as well as desaturation by enzymes in the mitochondria and membranes of the endoplasmic reticulum. In ER palmitate is elongated 2 carbons at a time by addition of malonyl at carboxyl end and its further Co-A is source for elongation and requires NADPH.

Mitochondria uses acetyl Co-A as source of 2 carbons. These reaction are essentially reverse of fatty acid catabolsim except NADPH use in saturation instead of FADH. Stearoyl Co-A desaturate at middle by stearoyl CoA desaturase to produce OleoylCo-A.

**Can mammals synthesize linoleic and linolenic acids?**

**Ans**- No. plants can introduce double bond between C-9 and $CH_3$ end of fatty acid but mammals can't. Plant easily desaturate oleic acid at 12 position to form linoleic acid or at both 12 and 15$^{th}$ to form linolenic acid. Mammals introduced double bond between 8/9 carbon and carboxyl group.

**Describe Pyruvate dehydrogenase complex.**

**Ans**- Pyruvate dehydrogenase complex (PDC) is a complex of three enzymesthat converts pyruvate into acetyl-CoA by a process called pyruvate decarboxylation.Acetyl-CoA may then be used in the citric acid cycle to carry out cellular respiration, and this complex links the glycolysis metabolic pathway to the citric acid cycle. Pyruvate decarboxylation is also known as the "pyruvate dehydrogenase reaction" because it also involves the oxidation of pyruvate.

- Pyruvate dehydrogenase (E1)

The E1 subunit, called the pyruvate dehydrogenase subunit, has a structure that consists of two chains .A magnesium ion forms a 4-coordinate complex with three, polar amino acid residues (Asp,

Asn, and Tyr) located on the alpha chain, and the thiamine diphosphate (TPP) cofactor directly involved in decarboxylation of the pyruvate.

- Dihydrolipoyl transacetylase (E2)

The E2 subunit, or dihydrolipoyl acetyltransferase, for both prokaryotes and eukaryotes, is generally composed of three domains. The N-terminal domain (the lipoyl domain), consists of 1-3 lipoyl groups of approximately 80 amino acids each. The peripheral subunit binding domain (PBSD), serves as a selective binding site for other domains of the E1 and E3 subunits. Finally, the C-terminal (catalytic) domain catalyzes the transfer of acetyl groups and acetyl-CoA synthesis.

- Dihydrolipoyl dehydrogenase (E3)

The E3 subunit, called the dihydrolipoyl dehydrogenaseenzyme, is characterized as a homodimer protein wherein two cysteine residues, engaged in disulfide bonding, and the FAD cofactor in the active site facilitate its main purpose as an oxidizing catalyst.

- Dihydrolipoyl dehydrogenase Binding protein (E3BP)

An auxiliary protein unique to most eukaryotes is the E3 binding protein (E3BP), which serves to bind the E3 subunit to the PDC complex. In the case of human E3BP, hydrophobic proline and leucine residues in the BP interact with the surface recognition site formed by the binding of two identical E3 monomers.

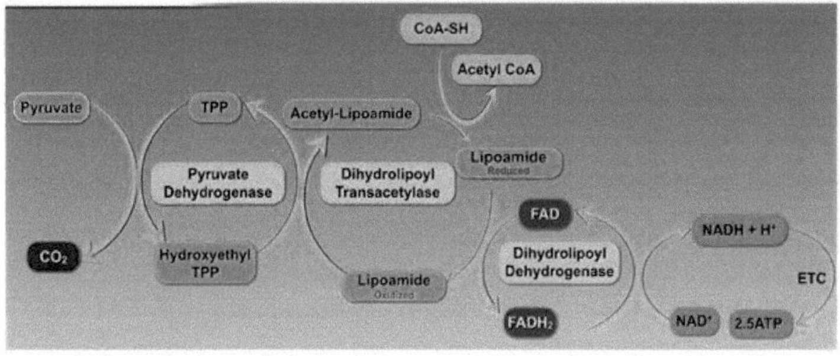


**The conversion of pyruvate to acetyl CoA is catalyzed by which enzyme?**

**Ans-** Pyruvate dehydrogenase.

**In TCA cycle, the reaction for the conversion of pyruvate to acetyl CoA is known as?**

**Ans-** Oxidative decarboxylation.

**Name regulators of pyruvate dehydrogenase?**

**Ans-** a) Calcium

b) Acetyl CoA

c) ATP

**Which enzyme catalyzes the condensation of acetyl CoA and oxaloacetate to citrate?**

**Ans-** Citrate synthase.

**Which enzyme catalyzes substrate-level phosphorylation i.e conversion of GDP to GTP?**

**Ans-** Succinyl CoA thiokinase.

**In Krebs cycle, when two carbon Acetyl CoA is oxidized to CO2, How much ATP is produced?**

**Ans-** 12

**Which enzyme of the TCA cycle catalyzes co-reduction of FAD+ to FADH2?**

**Ans-** Succinate Dehydrogenase.

# About The Authors

He had 20+ years of experience in wide area of research and development and teaching. He had experience in medical technology and diagnostic tools, Biochemical analysis, presentation tools and techniques, Science Quiz Master. As Quiz Master, he conducted many science quizzes competitions in various part of country. In the Quiz a new method was developed by incorporation of science films content in Quiz Questions for promotion of Science Films of Vigyan Prasar. He also visited Japan as part of scientist delegation from Indian during 2012. He participated in 6 trainings in DNA analysis, Empirical Approach, Revised National Tuberculosis control program, Safe water and Demographer training for health workers. Presently in Vigyan Prasar I am working as Scientist-D and published books Vigyan Yatra-Science Poetry Book in Hindi, My Journey in Science Communication, and a novel Tear Drop A Love Story by notionpress.com.

**Sachin C Narwadiya**

Dr R L Meshram is Assistant professor and Head Department of Biochemistry DRB SIndhu Mahavidyalaya Nagpur, MS. He did MSc. , M.Phil,. PhD (from CSIR-NEERI). He has Research and teaching experience of more than 12 yrs in R.T.M Nagpur University & SGB Amravati University. He was also former IGNOU Counsellor for Nutritional Biochemistry.

**Dr Rahul L Meshram**

Dr (Mrs) Damini Rakesh Motwani, Assistant professor at Department of Biochemistry. She did M.Sc,M.Phil, P.hd(Biochemistry) and B.Ed. She had three years teaching experience

**Dr (Mrs) Damini Rakesh Motwani**

Printed by Libri Plureos GmbH in Hamburg,
Germany